# THE LIAR'S QUARTET

Also by Mark Thomas from September Publishing:

*100 Acts of Minor Dissent*

*To Simon*

# MARK THOMAS

## THE LIAR'S QUARTET

*Love + peace*

## BRAVO FIGARO!

## CUCKOOED

## THE RED SHED

Playscripts, Notes and
Commentary

s
epte
m
b
er

X

1 3 5 7 9 10 8 6 4 2

First published in 2017 by September Publishing

Copyright © Mark Thomas 2012, 2014, 2016, 2017

*Bravo Figaro!* was first published by Mr Sands in 2012
*Cuckooed* was first published by Mr Sands in 2014
*The Red Shed* was first published by Mr Sands in 2016

Typeset by Ed Pickford
Printed in Denmark by Nørhaven

Printed in Poland on paper from responsibly managed,
sustainable sources by Hussar Books

ISBN 978-1-910463-69-7

September Publishing
www.septemberpublishing.org

# CONTENTS

# INTRODUCTION BY DR OLLIE DOUBLE

've been following Mark Thomas's work for the best part of thirty years. I first became aware of him in 1988, when he did a short spot on Channel 4's *Friday Night Live*, in which he started out by asking, incredulously, '*What – are they talking about – in opera?*' After taking the piss out of that venerated musical form, he went on to suggest that you could start a revolution by swapping the muzak in supermarkets for records by The Clash and The Damned, inciting the customers to riot. Meanwhile, you'd pump the muzak into police cars, making the officers within so docile that they'd observe the riot with benign disinterest.

A few months later I found myself on the same bill as Mark, at a comedy night in a snooker club in Coventry run by the theatre company TICTOC. Mark was top of the bill and I was a lowly open mike spot, and to say I was impressed would be an understatement. My abiding memory of that gig was of how he dealt with a persistent, drunk heckler. There used to be a standard ploy on the comedy circuit that if somebody like that went out to the toilet, the comedian would say to the audience, 'Let's all hide!' The audience would laugh at the very idea of playing such a prank on the heckler. On this occasion,

Mark actually followed through with it, persuading the entire audience of about 100 people to hide (behind some screens, I think), so that when the drunk returned he was faced with an empty auditorium.

In these early examples, all the things that make Mark's work so distinctive are there – politics, punk and an ability to take the audience somewhere they didn't expect to go. He has gone on to develop these envelope-pushing qualities in all the full-length shows he has created this century, whether it's finishing *Dambusters* (2001) with a furious, punchline-free rant about human rights abuses in Turkey, asking the audience for their suggestions for a better world in *It's the Stupid Economy* (2009), or playing the campaigning prankster in *100 Acts of Minor Dissent* (2013).

He is often pigeonholed as a political comedian, but just as important is his love of playing about with the form of stand-up comedy, and the three scripts collected in this volume are an excellent example of that. In each of these shows, Mark places stand-up into a more formal theatrical frame, particularly in the staging which incorporates sophisticated sets, lighting cues and recorded voices. In a long telephone conversation, I ask him about the politics and the key creative decisions behind them.

*Bravo Figaro* started after an appearance on BBC Radio 4's *Saturday Live* with Fi Glover. 'She said, "We've got this idea for a section called Inheritance Tracks, where people talk about the songs they inherit from their family and the songs they pass onto their family. We're doing loads of interviews for the first programme to see if we can get a story. Have you got anything?" And I told her the story of how my dad, who was a working-class builder, a self-educated man who left school with no qualifications, discovers a love of opera. And how embarrassing it was for me that he would play this music on the building site, because I'm a punk rocker!'

Mark also talked about the fact that his father had developed progressive supranuclear palsy, a degenerative illness which encompasses dementia. 'In an attempt to reach out to him, I found myself singing and remembering these arias. When I used to bath my daughter, I used to put soap between her toes and I would sing bursts of Figaro's aria from *The Barber of Seville*. And I talked about how I'd now started to go to opera, as a way to communicate with him, really.'

Somebody from the Royal Opera House heard the programme, and Mark was invited to meet Mike Figgis, who asked him if he'd like to develop a show about class and opera for a festival he was directing. Mark agreed: 'I said, "Alright, I will, but I want opera singers and I'm going to try and put an opera on in my dad's bungalow – because he can't get out, he can't move much." And he agreed to do it. So he lent me these opera singers and we rehearsed a programme of arias, and we did a performance in my mum and dad's living room in their bungalow in Bournemouth. And then, because my dad was really awakened by the event, I did interviews with him and my mum, and we had sound recordists with us so we could record them.'

About ten days before the show, Mark started to rehearse with the director Hamish Pirie and work on the material, and they realised, 'We've got something interesting here.' They showed this early version at the Royal Opera House Deloitte festival and the reception it received inspired them to develop it more fully, taking it up to the Edinburgh Fringe before touring it.

'I've always been pushing to do more stories,' Mark says. 'If you look back, you have *Dambusters*, which is a story. *Serious Organised Criminal* (2007), that's a full story. *Walking the Wall* (2011) is a story. They are narratives. And I love the idea of telling stories, but now there was a chance to tell a story in a theatrical way, that utilised all the dramatic devices to recreate it and show the truth of it – and get those other voices onto the stage. Because I think one of the interesting things about stand-up is the fact that it's you impersonating other people, but it's essentially your voice. So it's literally a question of how do you get other people onto the stage? Well, you record them and you play it. It was the most theatrical thing I'd done to date. I'd done stand-up. And then I was telling stories but still in the stand-up mode. And this was like a clean break into a much more theatrical way of doing it.'

It was also a break in the sense that it was the most personal show he had done. Yet there was still an under-lying political motivation: 'It sounds really weird, but it's about sticking my fingers up at the liberals. It's about celebrating a working-class Tory. My dad had more faults than you could shake a stick at, but there are things that he achieved in terms of his life and in terms of the idea of self-improvement. You might not like his politics, and you might not have liked him, but he fucking came from a bad place and ended up in a good place. And the idea of working-class self-improvement is one that's just forgotten.'

Undoubtedly, though, doing such a personal show surprised an audience that had come to know him as an overtly political comedian. 'What I like doing is defying expectation, I think we should all try and defy expectations to create new things. I love doing that. I think it's really exciting. For me, stand-up was the foundation. It's what I fell in love with and it gave me a certain set of skills, and I thought, "OK, where can we go with this? What can we do with this? How can we play with this? How do we make shows which are really different?" Because you know and I know that of all the comics we've seen in all the years, 90 per cent of it is wallpaper. Can you remember 90 per cent of the stuff you've seen? So how do you stand out in that? How do you go, "OK, here's something that you won't have thought of, here's something you won't have seen before, here's putting a spanner in the works to make you look at it again"? Playing with the form of it is really exciting.'

One way that *Bravo Figaro* plays with the form of stand-up is to expand its emotional palette, taking the audience through peaks and troughs of love and loss as well as allowing them to laugh at the gags. 'The thing about theatre is that it offers you the chance to empathise and feel emotions. All jokes are stories. There's a beginning, a middle and the wrong ending. That's how it works. Basically, this is taking that and just going, "Let's fill in the gaps, let's colour in what's in the rest of the story."'

\*

*Cuckooed* is a more overtly political show, telling the true tale of how Mark and fellow campaigners in the organisation Campaign Against Arms Trade (CAAT) had been spied on for years by a man called Martin – who they believed to be their friend and comrade but had been employed to spy for the arms company BAE Systems. In an era rife with stories about espionage perpetrated by governments, police, secret services and even – as in this case – corporations, this show has much to say about breaches of privacy and the exercise of power. However, like *Bravo Figaro*, it also explores emotion. Mark says, 'The thing that motivates you to do it is explaining complexities. I wanted to do a show that showed the emotional impact of the betrayal of being spied upon.'

Mark was close to Martin, and initially dismissed the suspicions that were starting to be raised about him. He even took Martin out on tour with him. This made it all the harder when he eventually saw the evidence which showed that his friend was actually a spy. 'I just stopped talking with him. That was it, we just dropped it. And I was really embarrassed and shamed. I think this thing with betrayal is it's the shame that exists in you that is generated. If there was any moral logic to the world, the shame should be generated in the betrayer. But actually it's the shame that you feel within yourself for having been deceived, for having not been clever enough, for not spotting the signs, for allowing it to happen.'

*Cuckooed*, like *Bravo Figaro*, incorporates the recorded voices of other people involved in the story. Mark's fellow campaigners gave video interviews which are seen on screens that appear when drawers of the filing cabinets in the set – a recreation of the CAAT office – are opened. Interacting with the recorded footage requires pinpoint timing, and I ask Mark how much the technical business of having to hit precise cues limits his ability to play and improvise as he would in a more regular stand-up show.

'I started to do the scripts because the technicians were demanding them. They were saying, "We need to know when to press the buttons." Tine, who has been my tour tech and manager for a while now, is amazing because she knows that actually the tightness and the rigour and the discipline happens within those exchanges on screen. And the stuff that happens around that – we have a series of points to get to, we have a story to tell, but there's always room to play, there's always things we'll add in, there's always bits that will be slightly different. And so there's a bit in the show where I'd play around with where the audience were at and it changed every night. There's a little bit where I directly address them as the audience. There's this idea that actually one can speak to the audience and you can speak to the audience in a whole fucking load of different terms and in a myriad of ways. But if you're actually addressing the now, addressing where we are right now, right here, in this room, in this place – you know, that's a different way of doing it. And we'd always have bits to play with, that would be in the show. And I like to think that we built into the structure of it a degree of playfulness.'

Like *Bravo Figaro*, *Cuckooed* was developed with a director. This time, Mark worked with Emma Callander. It's not unheard of for comedians to work with a director to create a full-length show, but it's still far from the norm, so I ask Mark how it changed things. 'I think the great thing about working with directors who are good – and both Emma and Hamish are very good – is the ruthlessness with which they approach questioning you and what you do. Why are you doing that? What is the truth? What is motivating you at this point? Why do you want to tell me this story and not another story? What's important about it? I think that working with them challenged how I work as a performer, and they were very rigorous in the method of how they did that. And that was really exciting. I really like working with directors, particularly the discipline of it. And the fact that you explore things that you might not have explored by yourself.'

*The Red Shed* explores something quite different, celebrating the Wakefield Labour Club – which, as the name suggests, is a wooden shed which is painted red. It was centrally important to Mark when he studied Theatre Arts at Bretton Hall in the 1980s because it was, 'The place where I started to perform in public and it is a place that's very important for me for the political awakening.'

The Red Shed was coming up to its fiftieth anniversary and Mark was asked to come up with some ideas for its celebrations. He responded by creating the show, which he did with the help of another director, Joe Douglas. Its central narrative arc begins with a memory of Mark's involvement in supporting the miners' strike of 1984–85. He recalled being in a pit village and seeing the miners marching back to work after the strike was over, while the children of the local primary school watched through the railings of the playground and sang 'Solidarity Forever'.

The problem was that although he had told the story many times, Mark couldn't be sure how much of it was true, so he set out to track down the village and the school in a quest to find out. The show tells the story of this quest. Mark says, 'The ideas of collective memory, of remembering and of working-class stories are really, really important, and we're in a state where we've lost an enormous amount of working-class identity. It's absolutely a quest show, it's absolutely about intervention, and I believe firmly in this: that when we tell stories, it's no good just repeating the old facts. We have to intervene to create the narrative.'

The form the show takes reflects its themes. Individual audience members sit on stage with Mark, holding up stick-masks with photographs of faces to represent the real people he talks about in the story, and the audience as a whole contribute by singing, whistling and letting off party poppers at key moments. 'I think that idea of community and community action is a brilliant and important thing. I wanted people in the audience to feel like the show couldn't exist without their help – that the show is made by the audience.'

One of the delights of seeing *The Red Shed* performed is that sometimes when something funny happens, we see the masks wobble and we realise that the punters holding them are laughing. Thus, we simultaneously see the characters Mark describes and the punter-performers who are playing them. 'We build up these layers. There's Pete and there's Sandra. There's also the person playing

Pete and Sandra. And the fun that we have on stage, it is about play, it is about that community. I love it when things go slightly wrong – or *right*, as I like to think of it. Somebody does something and you think, "Well that wasn't in the script but let's celebrate that!"'

As with *Bravo Figaro* and *Cuckooed*, *The Red Shed* uses the recorded voices of the people involved in the story, and I put it to Mark that this is an authenticating strategy. 'Yeah, I mean, if you've gone to the trouble of fucking doing all this research and running around the Yorkshire countryside with these people looking for a fucking school, people at least know it's fucking true. You're absolutely right, it is an authenticating strategy and it says, "this is true", but it's also a way of making other voices appear. Literally, other voices appear. And they lay claim to some of the story.'

*The Red Shed* is centred on events that took place over thirty years ago, but its political themes are very current in the era of Brexit, Donald Trump and the post-truth world. 'There is a battle of narratives. The working-class narrative is being erased. And as you erase that narrative, you erase truths with it. When Trump is literally trying to manipulate departments of state for disproving his narrative, it's a really fucking dangerous time. And so for me to do a show that is about the importance of working-class narratives is really exciting.'

I finish by asking Mark whether he feels, given the publication of these three scripts, that they could be restaged by other performers. 'One of the things about stand-up is how a stand-up has a persona – rather than a character. And the persona is very, very different. It's an amplified, selected version of yourself. So what I do is I play a persona in telling the story. I narrate myself, almost. Could another performer do it? Yes, of course they could. These are very tight structures and narratives. I think the people that play me should be slightly more handsome and thinner – to represent the inner me. And possibly younger.'

Dr Ollie Double
Deputy Head, School of Arts and Director of Comedy and Popular Performance
University of Kent
2017

*Each playscript and much of the original programme matter is printed verbatim, with new annotations for this collection.*

# BRAVO FIGARO!

# MY DAD AND I

I n the second week of March 2000, my dad, Colin Alec Todd Thomas, was diagnosed with a disease called Progressive Supranuclear Palsy (PSP) a degenerative and incurable condition, which is often misdiagnosed as MS. Now, he is nearly blind, can't walk, can barely talk, can't swallow properly, has diabetes and dementia and last week, my mum, his carer, was told she could add gout to the list. In most likelihood he will die of hyper-static pneumonia.* Frankly he was a grumpy bastard to begin with and none of this has improved his mood.

I have responded to witnessing this cruel slide downwards with the appropriate dignity and written a show about it for the Edinburgh festival, *Bravo Figaro!* now on tour. Book now while tickets last!

It's about my dad and me, love, death and opera. It came about as the result of a series of coincidences: an interview on Radio 4 about music led to a commission by the Royal Opera House, which became this show's starting point.

This much is true. Ish. True-ish. Like many performers I have plundered my family for inspiration over the years but the fuller truth of *Bravo Figaro!* started one Friday night

---

* Caused by the build-up of fluid in the lungs.

24 years ago when Ben Elton introduced me to a live TV studio audience.* Sweaty with fear I stared at the crowd, then mangling vowels in a youthful mockney accent indignantly shouted one word,

'What!'

I paused, waited, rode out a few titters, then glowering into the darkness continued,

'Are they talking about ...'

I paused again, held it, made the wait significant, then bellowed incredulously,

'... in opera!'

This opening line was the springboard for a torrent of filth sung fast and furious, a paean to obscenely bad sex,† belted out in alternating falsetto and tenor tones; thus reducing an entire art form to a series of grunts, shafts, shags and squelches.

Though not the stuff of legend the routine was then my calling card on the comedy circuit, regarded at best as comedic filth with a dash of righteous toff bashing. Hardly anyone knew that the routine was actually aimed very squarely at my dad.

Colin Alec Todd Thomas was a working-class Tory and self-employed builder who discovered a love of opera as an adult and like many a late convert his zeal burnt brightly. On Sunday mornings our neighbours were blasted with Rossini and Verdi played at such a level that even now I have an impulse to apologise. He even took a cassette player to work, playing his favourite operas across the

---

* *Friday Night Live*, 1988.
† Imagine Bryn Terfel Jones mid-Wagner eulogising on jism.

rooftops and building sites of south London. It was excruciating. As a teenager working alongside my dad I would cringe in embarrassment but I would be revenged when I spat and sung my way through my obscene parody of his beloved opera on national telly.

In social attitudes my father was born in the wrong century; he wanted a world where men were masters, women were quiet and children had rickets. When he said, 'They should bring back the death penalty and if no one else will do it I'll throw the switch,' not only did he mean it, but he would have brought his own set of jump leads and a car battery as back up.* It's not suprising that he was frequently the focus of my early routines and became a foil similar to the old-school comics of my youth who would parry at their mother-in-law.

However, over time my shows became increasingly political and theatrical and over that same period he became just slightly more tolerant. As the well of material he provided dried up so did my desire to draw from it. It was not my intention to return to my family as source material again. We had reached some kind of agreeable stand-off, I went off and did exposés on arms dealers and expounded the virtues of the right to protest and in return he stopped wincing every time a lesbian character appeared on TV.

---

* I did a show called *The Manifesto* where the audience could submit policy suggestions to create a blueprint for a better world and during the tour, at every single show, someone would submit 'bring back hanging'. I got so sick of it I eventually agreed. 'Fuck it, we should bring back hanging but let's do it on a voluntary basis. So if you agree with the death penalty, you sign up to a public register and then if you fuck up, we kill you.'

Ten years after the diagnosis, Colin Alec Todd Thomas sits in the corner of the room with his eyes shut, shaking, sweating and unable to remember what he had for lunch. I'm drawn to opera, the art form he loved, in an effort to reach out to him before he vanishes. So the decision to do *Bravo Figaro!* was more instinctive than rational but with so personal a story it raised the question of how I represent him onstage: should I treat him differently this time around because his time with us is short? Well, yes and no. Once again my dad is resolutely lambasted as there seems no point in telling so private a tale without trying to tell the truth ... and to be honest the stories of him being a bastard are comedy gold.

It is not all one sided and my dad speaks for himself in this show as audio interviews with him and my mum have been woven into the script and they help tell the stories. But there is one significant change in how I represent my dad this time around, thirty-odd years later, and it is this: now, the image of him standing on the scaffolding singing opera across the rooftops of south London is the image of him I cherish the most.

# FOREWORD

This is the first script I have written onto paper, which may possibly make it a play but don't be put off by that.

Normally I write shows by performing them, going to small venues and doing 'work in progress' shows to an intimate crowd. It is a trial and error process so the tickets are cheap and the audiences come on the understanding that I might be crap, some nights I am, just so they get their monies worth.

The scripts for these shows remain only as a series of headings, flow charts and single word aide memoirs. These aide memoirs are temporary and are worthless within eighteen months of the last performance of a show.

One old notebook has a twenty minute routine written in it. It reads: Alpha. Virgin. Dad. Book. Scopes Trial. Sabina Guzzanti. Pope. Erection.

If anyone can remember how that routine went please don't remind me.

*Bravo Figaro!* was scripted because people kept shouting at me. Technicians shoutest loudest, demanding to know when to play sound cues and turn lights on and off.

The Traverse Theatre,* being a theatre of new writing, thought it might be a good idea if there was some kind of script too.

Is it a play? Well, I like to think of it as a series of precise lighting and sound cues broken up with stories that might change from night to night.

One technician described it as 'a bit jazz', which I am assured could be an insult.

If *Bravo Figaro!* is a play, others can perform it, on condition they give me money.

The recordings of my mum (Margaret), my dad (Colin) and my brother (Matt) are real recordings and no actors of any kind were harmed in the making of them.

Mark Thomas
July 2012

---

* *Bravo Figaro!* was massively rewritten after its first outing at the Royal Opera House and opened in its current form at the Traverse Theatre during the Edinburgh Fringe. The Traverse was my first and only choice – it's a great venue, with a seriously brilliant tech and stage crew. Not to mention you're sharing a bill with a set of performers and writers who make you up your game.

# BRAVO FIGARO!

*Onstage left: To one side five packing boxes and a
sack barrow with boxsets of opera records piled on it,
an electrician's lamp\* hangs from it. A wooden lamp†
protrudes from another box and medical packages‡ are
stacked on another. Next to the sack barrow with records
is a small stool.*

*Onstage right: A wooden ark toy on wheels is surrounded
by toy dinosaurs.§*

*The electrician's lamp fades up when MT's dad speaks,
the wooden lamp in the box lights when MT's mum
speaks and the ark lights up whenever Matt speaks.*

---

\* The authenticity of the props was very important, the barrow
was actually my dad's old sack barrow. When the show opened in
Edinburgh we had a backdrop of a skirting board and wallpaper that
exactly matched what we had at home at the time, and a massive
frame into which we projected a picture of my dad.
† It's an old elephant lamp belonging to my nan. She left it to my mum
who gave it to me. The lamp is made of old hardwood, the statue is an
elephant lifting its head and trunk upwards and the bulb goes at the
end of the trunk. It's more likely to appear at a car boot sale than the
*Antiques Roadshow*. Before touring the show in Australia, my tour
manager removed the small remnants of a white tusk – just as well or
we would have been arrested for ivory smuggling.
‡ The actual packaging of my dad's medicines.
§ The dinosaurs were my children's.

*SFX: SCAFFOLDING CLUNKS, COMMER VAN
ENGINE AND ANGLE GRINDERS, WHISTLING
SLIGHTLY NONDESCRIPT AND OCCASIONAL
SNATCHES OF PUNK SONGS*

*The show starts with the sound of my dad breathing.*

*SFX: HARD AND LABOURED BREATHING*

*LIGHTS UP AROUND THE BOXES AND MT SITS
NEXT TO THE SACK BARROW.*

What did you think to the event, Dad?

*SFX: MUM AND DAD VOICES*

**DAD:** *BUILDER'S LAMP LIGHTS UP* **It was smashing –
really brilliant.**

**MUM:** *ELEPHANT LAMP LIGHTS UP* **It was brilliant.**

What did you enjoy about it?

**MUM:** *ELEPHANT LAMP LIGHTS UP* **I don't think he can
express himself, love.**

**DAD:** *BUILDER'S LAMP LIGHTS UP* **The music.**

Did you recognise the tunes, Dad?

**DAD:** *BUILDER'S LAMP LIGHTS UP. COUGHING* **All of
them, love.**

**MUM:** *ELEPHANT LAMP LIGHTS UP* **Eh?**

**DAD:** *BUILDER'S LAMP LIGHTS UP* **I recognised all of them.**

**MUM:** *ELEPHANT LAMP LIGHTS UP* **What was that? You recognised all of them – oh that was good, love.**

**DAD:** *BUILDER'S LAMP LIGHTS UP* **Yeah.**

This is what my mum and dad sound like and this conversation was recorded at the end of last year but let's start the story nearer the beginning.

I started performing in professional stand-up venues in 1985,[*] when poets, ranters, musicians street performers, circus performers, cabaret artistes, magicians, performance artists, the leftovers of left-wing theatre, the Manchester University drama department and anarcho counter-culture of squatters of Ladbroke Grove collided to create the white heat of alternative comedy.

In rooms above pubs you could see any combinations of acts, the first act could be a low wire act, the second a squeeze box orchestra and the third a performance artist trying to melt a massive block of ice with his body heat in twenty minutes in a homage to the myth of Sisyphus.[†]

My favourite was Bob Boyton,[‡] he performed in sharp suits

---

[*] Some of my fellow drama students may care to date the start of my stand-up career to performances at college, in particular the profound and moving 'fart sketch'.

[†] The Iceman – the *nom du guerre* of performance artist Antony Irving – is still performing but tends to paint more these days.

[‡] He's an ex-comic now, turned author and Camden tour guide and still a good friend.

and a fist full of sovereign rings, when he walked onstage half the audience thought he was a character comic. He would walk on holding the mic at a right angle, club comic style.

'Good evening ladies and gentlemen, my name is Bob Boyton and I'm a communist, Marxist Leninist. A lot of my comrades say football is the proletarian sport but that is bollocks. The proletarian sport is motor racing, few quid to get in, sit with your mates, a few beers, a nice day out and if you're lucky you watch some rich fucker burn to death.'

That was his opening gag! And I loved it because the audience were either on board the train and going the whole distance with Bob or you were leaving the room. At the time I had signed up to the alternative cabaret agenda. We believed that we were fighting a cultural war, against sexism and racism. We were fighting those who mocked the disabled, gays and immigrants. I was watching *Little Britain** and realized that we lost that war. Quite badly too. Our frontal attack on the conservative right left our flank completely exposed to postmodernism.

But, in the trenches of alternative comedy we attacked new targets, the bigots and the illiberal, mocking them for their hatred and stupidity. And there was no greater bigot that my father.†

---

\* When the show toured in New Zealand and Australia, the audience there were unfamiliar with *Little Britain*. I was left looking for an example of reactionary, boorish humour. It is the only time I have been thankful for the existence of Jeremy Clarkson.
† There were a lot of bigots to choose from in the 1980s – these were the days of James Anderton and Section 28.

## LIGHTS ON BOXES

Some of the music here was from *Tosca* ... do you remember going to see *Tosca*?

DAD: *BUILDER'S LAMP LIGHTS UP* Yeah, yes.

Do you remember where?

MUM: *ELEPHANT LAMP LIGHTS UP* Take that away from your mouth, darling, then they can hear you. Where did you go and see *Tosca*? Was it at Covent Garden?

DAD: *BUILDER'S LAMP LIGHTS UP* It was Covent Garden.

MUM: *ELEPHANT LAMP LIGHTS UP* He saw it at Covent Garden.

How long ago was that?

DAD: *BUILDER'S LAMP LIGHTS UP* Oh, forty-five years ago.

My father's name is Colin Alec Todd Thomas and I was born under the shadow of his character.

We used to say he looked like Moses with a hangover though not to his face. And when his beard went white we called him Santa with syphilis for variety.

My dad was a Wesleyan lay preacher,* a self-employed builder and the rudest man in south London – therefore Europe.

---

* My dad used to preach in the street in Clapham Junction and on Northcote Road. My uncle Norman told me that, as a young Teddy Boy, he once saw his mate sitting in front of my dad while he was preaching. My uncle bent over and asked him what he was doing. His mate replied, 'I've been saved.' Norman said, 'No, you fucking haven't, you're coming with me.'

He was a mass of contradictions and happy with them. Hypocrisy is what makes us interesting, frankly people who possess a unity of thought, word and action are the dullest fuckers to walk the earth. Hypocrisy is a humanising foible that is merely given a bad name by politicians.

He was happy with his contradictions. My dad was a religious man and righteous. He could recite the books of Bible literally backwards but watching him swear was to see a man shoot a thesaurus from the air and hear the words scream as they fall to earth.

He swore like a jazz bebop player, improvising around common themes. Fuck-arsehole-shit-wank-arsehole- bastard-fuck-shit-wank.*

He was essentially Cleo Lane with tourettes.†

He was quick with his fists and was fifty before he lost his first fight and came home with blood on his shirt.

There was a period of time when he was bound over to keep the peace on a yearly basis. He would do something silly, get bound over, make it to the end of the ban and then do something stupid and start again.

You remember the Moonies? Religious cult, big in the seventies. One year my dad had a theological dispute with the Moonies that resolved when he kicked them up the street. He was charged.

---

* This section is improvised on a nightly basis and cannot be regarded as word for word accurate – but you get the jist.
† One of my genuinely treasured memories of my dad is of him leaning out of the Commer van window and shouting, 'Oi Cuntybollocks!' It was something he did quite a lot while driving.

Now our next door neighbour at the time was a Salvation Army captain* – who for some reason liked my dad. When he heard of the court case he said,

'Would you like me to be a character witness?'

'That's great. Very kind.'

'Shall I wear the Salvation Army uniform?'

'Well it can't hurt.'

In court† the Salvation Army man stood in the dock and says,

'Colin Thomas is a good man, a family man, a God fearing man, honest trustworthy hardworking and a pillar of the community.'

We were sitting there going, 'I wish we knew this bloke, he sounds bloody great.'

My dad left school with no formal qualifications – it sounds trite but try doing it‡ – he did a four year apprenticeship in carpentry and joinery and then set up as a small works contractor, he became a self-employed builder.

He was old school. Everything had to be done the proper way. If a cupboard was to be made it had to be made the hard way – the proper way. That ark, *MT POINTS TO STAGE*

---

* My mum says they were called Betty and David and she used to give them a lift to the cash and carry.

† Magistrates' Court, Lavender Hill, Battersea.

‡ The situation has improved since his day. Back then, half of the working adult population in England and Wales had no qualifications. Now it's a fifth. A fifth. In the fifth largest economy in the world. In the twenty-first century.

*RIGHT AND ARK* my dad made that for me when I was one year old. That ark is forty-three years old. Alright, it's fifty but it could play forty-three.*

Everything had to be done the difficult way, if something had to be carried on site, he had to carry the heaviest load. If something was moved up a ladder he had to move fastest. When we were kids he put his hand through a buzz saw. Some said it was an accident, I tend to think it was showing off. 'I'm the best chippie in South London and I haven't even got five fingers!'

MATT: *ARK LIGHTS UP* I found them ...

This is my younger brother, Matt. I interviewed him separately from my mum and dad and I should explain that the emphasis is on *younger*.†

MATT: *ARK LIGHTS UP* I found them ...

You found Dad's fingers? When you were cleaning up the sawdust?

MATT: *ARK LIGHTS UP* I found his fingers.

What did you do with them?

---

* The ark is a large wooden boat on wheels, sturdy enough for a child's rough play. It looks a little more like a military landing craft than the vessel of two of every animal, which is entirely in keeping with my dad to create a paramilitary Bible toy. It survived the tour and is now in my office.
† He's eight years younger and a building site manager. In my best man's speech at his wedding I described how we used to share a bedroom as kids. I said we used to sleep in bunk beds and I slept on the top which I hated because I got motion sickness.

MATT: *ARK LIGHTS UP* I think I found quite a considerable bit of one finger and the tip of another and put them in a cigar box and took them up to Mum.

'You gave Mum a cigar box with Dad's fingers in it?'

When it comes to Mother's Day Clintons just don't cater for the imaginative child.*

Every family has its own stories and one of ours was that my dad was dyslexic though he could have been illiterate. Either way my mum would check all his paperwork because on more than one occasion a customer was offered 15 per cent DISOCUNT. Now if you are in the market for disocunt you want 100 per cent or nothing. You don't dabble in disocunt.

He had four kids and I was the eldest. Mark, Elisabeth, Ruth and Matt. All good biblical names.

My father rarely took us on holiday but one year he took his family of six on a narrow boat to the Coventry basin. Now at that time Coventry was a very industrialised area ... Sorry, for the younger members of the audience:

'industry' ... we used to make things and sell them and have communities. The by-product was pollution. The canal water was black with oil and chemicals.

One afternoon as he navigated the black waterways he was in a full blown Captain Hornblower reverie, sitting against the rail, tiller in his hand, when he heard this sound.

---

* After the accident, the third finger on his left hand came to a nail-less point and the tip of the first finger bent over like a hook, which he used to clean his ears with.

*SFX: SPLASH*

It was the sound of his wallet falling out of his back pocket. We had no credit cards and he turns to see the holiday money floating out across the water.

His instinctive and immediate reaction is to grab my sister Ruth who is eleven.

*MT MIMICS THROWING SOMEONE INTO WATER*
'Get the money!'

She is paddling through the black water towards the floating notes and smiling. The rest of us are, 'We want to go in!' So we all pile into the canal swimming in the black water and a dead dog floats past.

But that just about sums up my dad's relationship with everything, which was 'Get the money!'

*LIGHTS ON BOXES*

Would you call yourselves opera fans?

**DAD:** *BUILDER'S LAMP LIGHTS UP* **Yes.**

**MUM:** *ELEPHANT LAMP LIGHTS UP* **Well I suppose so, we like opera.**

Did many builders go to the opera?

**DAD:** *BUILDER'S LAMP LIGHTS UP* **No.**

Did you meet other people who were like you?

**DAD:** *BUILDER'S LAMP LIGHTS UP* **Don't think so, son.**

Did that put you off?

DAD: *BUILDER'S LAMP LIGHTS UP* No.

MUM: *ELEPHANT LAMP LIGHTS UP* Don't be daft.

My dad was imbued with a work ethic that went beyond mere Protestant; I have never understood why we got that as a religion; Catholics got drink, Mormons got sex, we got work. But you play the god you get dealt. Dad worked six days a week, ten hours a day and on Sundays did the paperwork and the scrap metal. Work defined him. There was no such thing as too much work. He was Thatcherite before she came along, work hard look after your family, and fuck everyone else. If you want anything you work hard and you pay for it.

Our lives were dominated by his work. He would get home at 6.30.

MATT: *ARK LIGHTS UP* He finished work at 6.30. Got home by about 7.

At 7 ... OK ... He would pull up the Commer van.

MATT: *ARK LIGHTS UP* I remember the van pulling up ...

... We all remember the van. My dad would gun the engine twice before turning it off. It was his way announcing to the neighbours, 'You were asleep when I started work, and you're having your tea when I get back, lazy bastards!'

This was our cue to go out to the van unload the rubbish put it in the skip, shot the scrap metal down the side and stack the wood by the cellar hatch. My dad would come in for tea, dunk his hands in an enormous tin of Swarfega by the sink, a thick green industrial soap and he would turn it black with the oil and grime of the day. Then join his hands and say 'Our Father Who Art in' ... After tea we would cut and stack the wood. Then we could relax.

Now my dad always had his bath in the morning so he was clean for work, which meant he spent the evening unbathed and in his work clothes as a romantic gesture for my mum. When he would watch telly he was always worried that he would get the dirt from his work clothes onto his favourite leather armchair. So he would switch on the telly, drop his trousers and sit in his long johns with his trousers round his ankles laughing at *Steptoe and Son*. For younger members of the audience *Steptoe and Son* was a sitcom about a father and son trapped in a relationship of mutual mistrust and embarrassment ... anyway ...

If someone called at our house after the telly had gone on and Dad had sat down you would hear two sounds.

*SFX: DOORBELL*

Followed by my dad, 'Suppose I better put me trousers on.'

MUM: *ELEPHANT LAMP LIGHTS UP. LAUGHS* Not a good image is it, darling?

DAD: *BUILDER'S LAMP LIGHTS UP. LAUGHS* No, not really.

MUM: *ELEPHANT LAMP LIGHTS UP* He was a night-mare, wasn't he?

Nightmare ... He was forever collecting bloody scrap metal.

MUM: *ELEPHANT LAMP LIGHTS UP* Him and Mack could not pass a skip without him mooching into it to see if there was anything.

He was a totter.

MUM: *ELEPHANT LAMP LIGHTS UP* Yes, he was a totter.

He did well for himself financially too and when I was eleven I plucked up courage to ask him, 'Dad, are we middle class yet?'

'No we are fucking not!'

It offended him to be even asked.

He was working class and his children were going to be educated but not so they could be middle class, he didn't want us to be middle class he wanted us to be rich! Filthy fucking rich. I've been somewhat of a disappointment. On both counts.

This is the big difference between middle class and the working class. Middle-class parents want their children to be like them, to have the same opportunities they had. Working-class parents want better for their kids, they wanted them to be improved, they want their kids to look down at them and to that extent my dad has been successful.

I know some of you will say, 'Oh Mark, you bang on about class but we are all middle class now' – well tell your cleaner, I am sure she will be delighted.*

---

\* There are 13.5 million people in the UK living in poverty, over half of them from working families and 2.6 million of them children.

If you are unsure what class you are, there is a simple test: if someone says, 'Pass the olive oil' and you say, 'Which one?' you're middle class.

If you use the word 'distressed' to describe relatives rather than furniture you're working class. 'Your table's distressed? You should see my nan at the self-service checkout, that's distressed.'

I am resolutely middle class though I put myself in the bohemian bracket. Essentially if John Lewis had a tattoo parlour, I would be first in the queue, 'I'd like crossed lemon zesters and a honeycomb please.'

What my dad *disliked* about the middle classes was that he thought they were smug and pretentious but what he *hated* was their aversion to physical labour. Sure he would fix your house and he would fix it brilliantly too.

MATT: *ARK LIGHTS UP* **The man was amazing with a hammer and a fucking chisel.**

He was a craftsman.

MATT: *ARK LIGHTS UP* **He was beautiful with it.**

He would roll his sleeves up and get his hands dirty for you and make you something of beauty. And you could look down at him when he talked about Maggie and how great she was and he dropped his H's and effed and blinded but he would earn more than you ever would.

*SFX: OPERA BURST*

In a way it was not that surprising that he should discover a love of opera.

*SFX: OPERA BURST*

The richest art form, the most elitist art form, the most exclusive art form, the most expensive one.

*SFX: OPERA CONTINUES TO PLAY UNDERNEATH*

It was in another language and it was simply not something for someone like him. Opera is the default culture setting for the ruling class. It is where they go instead of karaoke. It was simply something that was not in his life.

He discovered opera partly through church music, as choral music often has a classical bent, but mainly through his belief in education. Education was not just for his children but himself, he believed in self-education and improvement. To that end every week my dad would get this ...

*HOLDS UP COPY OF* THE GREAT COMPOSERS

... this is *The Great Composers,*[*] a week by week guide to the great musicians and their music. It is a guide through classical music in alphabetical order starting with Bach and

---

[*] You can buy the complete collection – fifty-two records, plus the bonus opera highlights (thirteen records) and a Christmas special on eBay. I have my dad's entire set which also managed to survive the tour.

going through to Wagner. It cost thirteen pounds and ten shillings for a six-monthly subscription and you'd collect it from the local newsagent up the road. This is Mozart part five. Inside is a booklet like a theatre programme explaining the composer, contextualising the work, so we have articles on 1782–86 Hard Work of Mozart and Mozart and the Orchestra and here at the back is a sleeve and inside the sleeve is this.

*HOLDS ALOFT 10 INCH RECORD**

*SFX: OPERA BURST*

For the younger members of the audience ... this ... is vinyl and once upon a time we were very very fucking attached to it.†

Once there was a time when every great piece of music started with this sound ...

*SFX: SOUND OF NEEDLE GOING ON TO RECORD RUNNING INTO OPENING BARS OF DR FEELGOOD'S 'ROXETTE' (LIVE)*

The needle went through the grooves producing such a sound as would make us sway and tap and move our bodies in utter joy.

---

\* This was the only artificial prop we used. The sleeve was real but the record wasn't the original – I couldn't risk it getting damaged.
† Since writing and performing this, it seems vinyl is having something of a renaissance – hurray! I am taking complete credit for this change in fortunes. It was me and nobody else.

*MT DANCES UNTIL SFX OF NEEDLE BEING
SCRATCHED OFF A RECORD*

Every week my dad would get his copy, put it on the record player, sit down and read the programme notes, forcing himself to listen to the music, forcing himself to be improved ... with his trousers round his ankles.

*TURNS TO THE BOXES*

Do you remember the *Great Composers*, Classic series?

MUM: *ELEPHANT LAMP LIGHTS UP* The Classic series yes ... basically that is all we could afford at the time, wasn't it.

DAD: *BUILDER'S LAMP LIGHTS UP* Mostly classical music not a lot of opera but opera amongst it.

Was this the first time you would have heard some of those composers?

DAD: *BUILDER'S LAMP LIGHTS UP* Yes, a lot of times.

MUM: *ELEPHANT LAMP LIGHTS UP* Probably it was.

What were the bits that stood out for you?

DAD: *BUILDER'S LAMP LIGHTS UP* Rossini ...

Rossini?

DAD: *BUILDER'S LAMP LIGHTS UP* ... and Verdi.

Rossini and Verdi.

Here is a man whose entire self-image is constructed around his masculinity, who defines the word machismo, who has no fear of violence and a love of hard labour, for whom the words 'brute force' are an accolade. Who falls in love with an art form inhabited by sprites and elves, magic flutes, star-crossed lovers, gypsies singing of bullfighters, men in antlers and evil dukes. It is as if he stumbled across the shattered wasteland of his emotional life and in the stunted debris and weeds of his feelings found a box marked OHHHW! It was as if he had found his inner camp.

Opera left me cold. It was just panto for posh folk. Might as well put Christopher Biggins in a Pavarotti mask and shove him onstage. The worst thing about opera is if you go and see it you have to sit next to people who like it.

My dad loved it and every Sunday when he would do the paperwork the house became full of the sound of sopranos and tenors and Rossini's basses. Then he started to go to see it. Do you remember the first opera you saw?

DAD: *BUILDER'S LAMP LIGHTS UP* Yeah, love, *La Bohème.*

*La Bohème.* At Covent Garden. He got tickets in the slips so he had to stand. We said good job, because if he had a seat, he would sit down, hear the music and have to drop his trousers to get comfortable.

He took my mum all over the place to see the opera. Royal Opera – very classy, English National at the Coliseum – better 'cos it was in English. Glyndebourne, pricey but worth it. My mum remembers the first time she went to

Glyndebourne. She said, 'I sent your father up to the bar to get a glass of iced coffee and all I can hear is his voice going "How much?!"'

He knew his stuff too. He could tell you if he had seen a good opera or a bad one, unlike 80 per cent of the audience who are content just to pat themselves on the back for turning up. He loved the music but my mum said that was only half of it, what he really liked was dressing up, standing in his bow tie and cigar and a look on his face that said, 'I'm as fucking good as you.'

My dad would buy two sets of every opera, one would be the boxset in vinyl for home and the cassettes for work.* I'll say that again, cassettes for work. He took a tape recorder to work to play opera. So in the summer we would stick up the scaffold, tie it in, strip the slates, felt and baton, insulate and re-slate.† All the while my dad would be singing along to Rossini's *Barber of Seville* – 'Figaro's Aria'. My dad sung with the gusto of a Welsh male voice choir and the precision of the carpet bombing of Cambodia. Across the skyline of south London. He didn't know the words, so he would just improvise.

*SINGS FIGARO'S OPENING ARIA BADLY*

---

* If cassettes ever make a comeback, I'm claiming the credit for that too.

† As kids, we never had pocket money and I always worked for my dad to earn cash. The first time I was eight and he paid me 10p an hour for filling skips with rubbish. The neighbours said it was slave labour. He told them to fuck off. I spent my wages on cream soda and comics.

I am a sixteen-year-old punk. In an 'Anarchy and Freedom' t-shirt. To withstand that level of embarrassment you would need to be George Galloway.*

But the blokes on the site didn't take the piss. Only once did I see it. A friend of his called Mack, sitting downstairs for tea had heard the music all morning and said, ''kin' hell. What you fucking got up there, you stuck some bird on a pole or something?' My dad replied, 'I'll stick you on a pole in a minute, you uncultured prick.' And thus the debate ended.

Now at this point you might like my dad, think he is a character: a rough diamond, a wild card, a ruffian but with an inner heart of art and beauty, as he likes opera. In reality he was a cunt. He worked all hours, was rarely home so we hardly saw him and when he was, we were walking on eggshells least we did something to upset him. The fists that were quick to fly outside the home were just as quick to fly inside. Once one of the kids wrote the word 'bum' on the banister – which is the title of any future autobiography, *Bum on the Banister* by Mark Thomas and Noel Coward – so he lined us all up and hit all four of us until we cried and said, 'The one that has done it has been punished.'

MATT: *ARK LIGHTS UP* I know for a fact that once he lost it you didn't want to be anywhere near him. He did have a temper on him.

---

* For the New Zealand tour, we changed this to the then PM, John Key, who's a real knob. He's nicknamed 'Teflon John' as no scandal could stick. I've forgotten who we did in Australia. If I was performing this now, I'd replace Galloway with Boris Johnson, who is currently the most shameless twat in the UK.

**I don't like talking about it because he is my dad and I love him ... but he was a little bit punchy at times, weren't he?**

There was a stage when we would have an annual reunion at the accident and emergency where my mum had ended up on the end of one of those quick fists.

So when I say he was a cunt I am not saying it for effect. I mean it.

But this is not a story of a father finding a son's love, this is not a story of redemption, this is not a story of forgiveness. Those of us that have had cause to forgive him, forgave him a long time ago or we have learnt to live around it. I can't speak for the rest of my family, if you want to know what they think you'll have to go and see their shows, but for me this is a story about a gift.

Children have a way of finding the cracks and weakness of their parents. I know a man who is a doctor, he sounds like he fought in World War II and he did.* He was in the Navy. He runs a medical charity training doctors in the poorest parts of the world to the highest international standards. I like that. It means the poorest parts of the world get the best trained doctors. He phones up one afternoon and says,

'Mark we are having a fund raiser and I wondered if you might come and do some after dinner speaking?'

---

* The man in question is Colin Green. He still runs IMET2000 raising funds for medical training in Palestine. His work is so well known and respected that within days of the show opening, someone had recognised him, despite me not naming him, and grassed me up. He phoned and said, 'I hear I'm in your show and you've made me out to be a bloody toff.' We are still friends despite my impersonation.

'Well I don't really do after dinner speaking.'

'Oh ... oh never mind ... We are raising funds for the burns unit in Gaza ...'

*PAUSE*

'Look I'm sorry I can make something work. I'll do something for you.'

'Excellent. Thank you so much.'

'Where is it?'

'The House of Lords.'

I've done a gig in the House of Lords dining room. The only way to keep sane was to start by saying, 'Ladies and Gentlemen, my Lords and Ladies lovely to be here before we abolish you.'

Now the invite said 'Dress – casual lounge' which I do not possess – and even if I did I wouldn't admit it – but what I do posses is a Crombie – for lovers of youth culture of yesteryear you will know it is a long coat, nice velvet collar, red satin lining and a folding over for the buttons on the outside. Officially it is known as 'tasty schmutter'. I'm wearing the Crombie, a button-down shirt, Sta Press trousers and loafers. I am looking good. I am looking a little bit *This is England*[*] but I am looking good. I walk downstairs and my sixteen-year-old son says, 'Wow you look like you are dressed for a funeral.'

'Actually I am doing a gig at the House of Lords ...'

---

[*] If you don't know the reference, just Google 'skinhead fashion'.

'A funeral for your own dignity, father.'

Kids have a way of getting their own back on their parents. In my family, education and hard work were the most important weapons in the battle of aspiration. I was the first member of my family to go to university. To study drama.

He was proud and crestfallen in equal measure. Often within nanoseconds of each other. It is not that he was unsupportive, it was that everyone he spoke to seemed to say, 'Well it's very hard to make a living in that game.' And he was baffled as to why I should do so much studying for something with so little financial reward.

I loved it. It was Brecht and drugs and rock and roll. I remember coming home after my first term and running around to see my dad at work.

'Father, I have returned from university, come see, I have leg warmers. Father let me show you a Jacobean jig and round. Father, where are you going?'

But ever since I was sixteen I wanted to be a stand-up comic. My mum and dad kept away from the gigs for the first two years, which was fine because a lot of material was about them. But I also kept them away. The fourth gig I ever did was at a place called the Tunnel,* a notorious venue for open spots. I had done three gigs that had gone moderately well but I fancied myself a new Billy Connolly.

---

* It was by Rotherhithe tunnel and run by the late, great Malcolm Hardy, who compered the show. At some point in every performance he ever did he would play the harmonica after cleaning it in someone's beer and expose his genitals with the words, 'Oi oi nob out.'

I asked my brother-in-law and my sister to give me a lift to the gig where I was booed off. In the car park afterwards my brother in law said, 'Never invite me to one of your gigs again.'*

'Why not? It wasn't you getting booed.'

'No it was you they were shouting fuck off at. It was you they were chucking stuff at but it was your sister standing on a chair in the middle of the crowd shouting, "Shut up you slags, give him a fucking chance!" And it is not her they hit.'

The first stand up show my parents saw me perform at was on a pub boat that ran a cabaret evening. After the show my mum came up to me and said, 'Well you were better than the other two, they were shite.'

They would come along from time to time. My first one-man show I walk onstage and at that time started the show by saying, 'Look I never know how to start a gig these days.'

From the back of the room a voice goes, 'Get fucking on with it!'

Followed by my mum's voice hissing, 'Colin.'

And you have to explain to the audience, 'That's my dad. My mum and dad copulated twenty-seven years ago so they could arrive at this moment of hellish embarrassment.'

---

* My brother-in-law kept his word. My sister came to see this show. She was spotted by my tour manager sitting in the back of the theatre with her son on one side and second husband on the other holding a box of tissues, giving a running commentary of, 'that's true … that happened' throughout the show.

Ten years ago my dad started to walk backwards.

*SFX: CLOCK TICKING*

His feet would shoot out from under him and propel him in the wrong direction. He would lean forward to try to counteract the momentum, then his arms would shoot out and he would cry, 'OWWAY!' and fall over.

Over the months the falls got worse.

**MUM: *ELEPHANT LAMP LIGHTS UP* He could fall up to ten times a day.**

Then he started to shake.

**MUM: *ELEPHANT LAMP LIGHTS UP* That's right. When that arm went he had a kind of tremor to it and that was when I sent him to the doctor.**

He was diagnosed with progressive supranuclear palsy – PSP.*

Progressive because it is degenerative and worsening condition, so now you know the Lib Dems use the word its medical sense. Supranuclear as it is a neuroglogical disorder

---

* It's sometimes known as Steele-Richardson-Olszewski syndrome and is more often found in post-mortems than through diagnosis. Around one to six people in every 100,000 are estimated to have it. The average life expectancy after diagnosis is seven years. It's the same disease Dudley Moore had as well as Dr Ann Turner, who ended her life in a clinic in Switzerland and whose story was told in the drama, *A Short Stay in Switzerland*, where Ann was played by Julie Walters.

and a palsy is a weakening of the muscles. Progressive supra-nuclear palsy – it is sometimes misdiagnosed as MS – there is no treatment for PSP.

This is what happens. Movements start to slow down ...

MUM: *ELEPHANT LAMP LIGHTS UP* **Their balance is crap ...**

... there are frequent falls, clumsiness ...

MUM: *ELEPHANT LAMP LIGHTS UP* **He can't swallow properly ...**

... he can't walk ...

MUM: *ELEPHANT LAMP LIGHTS UP* **He can't talk ...**

... the muscles in his eyelids collapse ...

MUM: *ELEPHANT LAMP LIGHTS UP* **he can't see properly.**

Then there is the personality changes – irritation, grouchi-ness, memory loss, forgetfulness, apathy (indifference), slowed thinking, reasoning, planning, inappropriate laughing or crying – emotional incontinence with angry or aggressive outbursts.

Dementia accompanies this so as his body wanes and the muscles collapse his mind caves in. Leaving him immobile with a head skewed.

And the final indignity – my mum and dad move to Bournemouth. No, alright you're dying but you don't have to announce it to everyone. There are signs in the town with 'Bournemouth twinned with ERRR'. There are passengers on the train to Bournemouth with a return ticket and you think, 'That is optimistic.'

It is a five-hour return journey to Bournemouth and I don't get down there enough to see the day-to-day changes happening in my dad.

My mum was born around the corner from my dad, she trained as a nurse and did her midwifery in Glasgow, came back and married my dad, had kids and once we were up and running she ran a Spar – a proper one with an 'R' at the end and not a 'health' at the front. It was called Booze and Food and was robbed twice.

My mum refuses to put my dad in a home until she can no longer care for him. When I go to interview her about the changes in Dad she is twitchy.

*SITS ON END BOX AND TURNS TO HALF FACE THE WOODEN LAMP*

I ask her something like, 'But he is still the same person?'

**MUM:** *ELEPHANT LAMP LIGHTS UP* **Do you think he is?**

No but it's not about what I think it is about what you think.

**MUM:** *ELEPHANT LAMP LIGHTS UP* **Do you think it is? When you come down and see him sitting there and he might nod or he might smile. I doubt it.***

---

* He still recognises us.

Sometimes she is evasive.

MUM: *ELEPHANT LAMP LIGHTS UP* Would you?

Or just cross.

MUM: *ELEPHANT LAMP LIGHTS UP* No that is a cop out.

But she was a nurse and when I ask her a direct question she responses directly.

Do you think you know what will kill dad?

MUM: *ELEPHANT LAMP LIGHTS UP* He'll probably go with hypostatic pneumonia or something like that.

What's that?

MUM: *ELEPHANT LAMP LIGHTS UP* Because he doesn't swallow properly sometimes he gets these bouts of coughing because something has gone down the wrong way.

That's what will kill him?

MUM: *ELEPHANT LAMP LIGHTS UP* Yeah it usually does. It's usual in these kinds of cases.

But after a while she does open up and start to talk about the changes happening in my dad.

MUM: *ELEPHANT LAMP LIGHTS UP* If he was aware of what he does now like if he wets the bed or he does things, he'd be mortified normally.

When I come down here I try and see characteristics in him. I try and see something about him that links the old him to the new him.

MUM: *ELEPHANT LAMP LIGHTS UP* No this isn't your father it's just the shell of the person that we are just going through rituals with.

What do you mean?

MUM: *ELEPHANT LAMP LIGHTS UP* You could give him last week's paper to read and it wouldn't make any difference.

So he has lost his grip on reality?

MUM: *ELEPHANT LAMP LIGHTS UP* He had the same book for a year and it fell to pieces. So we took it away and gave him another one. It's like a comfort blanket.

About six years ago I was bathing my daughter, who was five at the time. I had soaped up my hand to wash her legs and feet and was about to wash in between her toes when from nowhere I suddenly find myself going,

'A bravo Figaro! Bravo, bravisimo.'

She is as surprised as I am. 'Do it again!'

And it becomes a ritual, whenever I bath her she says, 'Are we doing the Bravo song?'

'A bravo Figaro! Bravo, bravisimo.'

Then one night she says, 'No, no more, I'm not that girl any more. I've changed.'

And that was that.

One afternoon I am walking down Oxford Street, a beautiful sunny day when without a thought I walk into a shop and say, 'Have you got the Bravo Figaro opera, the Verdi?'

'Rossini.'

'The Rossini.'

I get the opera home and I don't know what to do with it. I played it on a Sunday afternoon while doing the VAT receipts, because we're not all Jimmy Carr.*

The first opera I went to see was shit. By the end of it two thirds of the cast are dead onstage and if they had asked me halfway through I would have helped out. I go to the comic operas, the light operas, the music is fine but the comedy is the most insufferable bourgeois shite imaginable.

'Oh the professor has caught his monocle in the harpsichord, how very very funny.'

And you just get this stabby stabby feeling.

I talk to my mate PD,† he is an eighteen-stone tour manager, an East End boy who has worked every West End theatre including the Coli and the Cov. He knows a lot about opera because he has shifted scenery on most of it. He says, 'Nah, I won't listen to opera now. It's all shit, except for John Adams, *Nixon in China* – fucking brilliant.'

And he is right, *Nixon in China* is amazing. John Adams' opera *The Death of Klinghoffer* is one of the most amazing things I have seen, an opera about the hijacking of the Achille Lauro, using contemporary history as the basis for

---

* Jimmy Carr is Britain's premier tax dodging satirist. Gary Barlow was involved in a similar offshore scam but he is a Tory and a patriot so we expected it of him.
† Real name Paul Delaney.

high art, using reportage in the opera and all set to modern minimalism. Amazing.

I start to take my son to the opera. I say to Paul, 'I am taking him to Don Giovani.'

'Good entry level opera. Mozart, like salmon. Very hard to fuck it up.'

I go and see Britten. Amazing brilliantly British sound within what is essentially a foreign art form. Puccini, *Madame Butterfly*, first act, good. Second amazing. Third felt like I had been run over by a steam roller. Wagner, *The Flying Dutchman*, two-and-a-half hours of listening to a tool being passed. Some opera is brilliant some is shit. Sometimes it is brilliant and shit in the same opera. But that's ok because if you don't doze off it's not really opera.

I end up going to the same places my dad went to. I go to Covent Garden and see *Salome*, Strauss doing Oscar Wilde doing John the Baptist, how can that miss? English National Opera, I see *Gaddafi the Opera*, it is shit as it sounds. I end up at Glyndebourne, the poshest opera house. I am late for the bell and I am running through in my dinner jacket but forgot my shoes so I am wearing Doc Martens boots and a 'Fuck the War' badge. As I run through the bar someone says, 'Good lord, is that Mark Thomas?' and I turn round and go, 'Yeargh' *THUMBS UP AND GRINNING* I am a cigar away from saying, 'I'm as fucking good as you.'

I get asked to meet the director and occasional opera director Mike Figgis.

So we meet in his studio, lots of camera equipment and a director's chair in one of those dockland warehouses. Nice fellow who strangely manages to have more and yet less hair than Art Garfunkel at the same time.

He said, 'Look I've been asked to curate a festival at the ROH and I wanted to work around the theme of 'tell the truth' just tell the truth! It seems to me that this is what people want, whether it is politicians or press or police or banks. Just tell the bloody truth! SO that is the theme and we have a variety of art forms appearing, we have dance, music, we have a discussion with the fashionistas on society, politics, fashion and gender AND I have done an interview with the art critic John Berger, lives in France won't come back, filmed the interview and am going to play it on a large screen in the Opera House. First thing he says is, 'You know I physically can't abide the rich, I can't even be in the same room as them.' Marvellous interview. Now do you think there is something you could do for the festival at the Royal Opera House around the idea of 'tell the bloody truth'?

'Yes. Yes, I think there is but I want opera singers. Proper ones from the Royal Opera House.'

'In the performance?'

'Sort of. Not really. I just want to borrow them.'

'I'll see what I can do.'

A plan is hatched and I get my pocket full of sopranos.

*SFX: PHONE RINGS TWICE. DOG BARKS. MUM'S VOICE*

**Get out of it!**

*WALK AND RUB HANDS. START SLOW AND END HIGH*

'Mum, first born, I've got this idea, don't shoot it down hear me out. Dad doesn't get out much, doesn't listen to opera and can't watch it on DVD. Mum I've got these opera singers, proper opera singers from the ROH. What would it be like if we did an opera for Dad in the living room? If we did a concert for him in the bungalow?'

My mum's first reaction is, 'Oh my God, what will the neighbours think?!'

She has got reservations so I leave her a few days.

*SFX: PHONE RINGS ONCE. DOG BARKS. MUM'S VOICE*

**Get out of it!**

'First born, Mum, it is really important to me that we try and make this concert happen, I know you have problems with it so let's talk them through one by one.'

'Well what if he goes to the loo?'

'What?'

'He can be in there for hours and nothing will shift him. The singers will have come all the way from London and he'll be stuck on the bog.'

'Mum that will be fine, we can take him to the loo in advance.'

'Well what about the ceiling?'

'What?'

'The ceiling is too small Mark, it's a bungalow with a low ceiling. The singers have got big voices and they need big ceilings.'

'Mum it will be fine ...'

'I'll have to do a buffet ...'

'What?'

'I know these opera singers they like to eat.'

'Fine do a buffet ...'

'And would it be alright for the nextdoor neighbour to come along? He's as deaf as a pisspot but he does love his music.'

'Yes I am sure that will all be fine. Can we do it?'

'Yes.'

'Are you going to tell Dad?'

'Not yet love he'll forget, we'll tell him nearer the time.'

I meet the singers. I rehearse with the singers. My dad is told, time passes. The day of the concert arrives and my mother has laid on the finest selection of cold meat platters known to Marks and Spencer. There is ham of every kind, there is roast, honey glaze, mustard seed and pancetta; sausages, sausage rolls and saucisson, pickles, gherkins, silver onions, pickled onions and piccalilli – or as my wife calls it 'working-class yellow food' and we have celery in a jug in the centre of the table. In an operation reminiscent of the Berlin airlift my dad is taken to the loo well in advance.

We've moved the furniture to one end of the living room creating a little performance space at the other end of the room where there are a pair of sliding doors.

So the audience, us, will sit in front of the fireplace and face the sliding doors that lead into the kitchen. The singers will enter through the sliding doors via the meat platters.

The hire piano has been delivered and is set up. The bungalow is hoovered and jiffed. My mum bustles and bristles with hospitality. The singers arrive and my mum goes out to meet them, saying what she always does, 'Welcome, welcome.

MUM: *ELEPHANT LAMP LIGHTS UP* This is the Mad House.

This is the Mad House.

And,

MUM: *ELEPHANT LAMP LIGHTS UP* Help yourself to whatever.

Help yourself to whatever.

Everyone comes in and the bungalow is full.

*SFX: BACKGROUND CHAT FROM THE CONCERT*

The talk is small and the drinks are large and the singers go into the living to meet my dad who has accidentally sat on the TV remote and the widescreen TV has two words on it 'ADULT CHANNEL', not words you want to see on a telly in a room with a large man shaking in the corner.

ROH have done playbills for the concert and hand them out.

They list the arias. Starting with Verdi, the 'Brindisi' from *La Traviata* and finishing with Puccini, *Tosca* and *La Bohème*.

## PROJECT THE PLAYBILL

The attic of the bungalow is converted to the singers' dressing rooms and they warm up upstairs, running through scales and it all seems very familiar.

Robert the next-door neighbour comes around.

My mum says, 'You look smart Robert.'

'What?'

'You look SMART.'

'Smart?'

'Smart.'

'SMART.'

Sophie from the ROH is co-ordinating the singers and she whispers, 'Is he the neighbour?'

'Nah the reviewer.'

We sit in the living room anxiously. My brother Matt has work so can't be here, but my sister Liz is, there is my mum and dad, Robert and the nephew, nieces and my son are all on a three-line whip. They sit in the second row of seats or as we call it the bungalow's middle stalls.

We sit clutching the playbills, my mum leans round to the kids sitting behind, 'Now you lot best behaviour don't embarrass me.'

Sophie clutches the playbill and looks on attentively.

The pianist walks through the sliding doors and bows, the dog* bounds over and shoves its snout into her crutch, my mum hisses, grabs the dog and singers enter through the sliding doors to a backdrop of cold meat and start to sing the 'Brindisi'.

*SFX: SINGERS SING THE 'BRINDISI'*

The singers seem to pitch the songs right at my dad, almost ignoring the rest of us. Hurling the notes at him as if willing him to be with us, to be present.

My mum is right. The ceiling is too low.

My son Charlie is filming with his camera from over my shoulder, Sophie from the Royal Opera House holds the playbill still. And my mum is smiling, one hand on her lap, the other clasped around the dog's snout with a grip a python would be proud of.

---

* Zeeli. A golden retriever inherited from a family friend who couldn't look after him any more.

My dad. His mouth is agape holding the arms of his chair forcing himself upright. His face is red with concentration, his white hair stands out against his complexion. But his eyes. He has fought with the eyelids that are closing and won. His eyes are open and I had forgotten they are blue. They are crystal blue. He is with us. He is back in the room.

*SFX: APPLAUSE AS SINGERS FINISH**

The applause is somewhat teary.

Everyone moves into the kitchen for the buffet. My dad stays in the living room, as he is being fed by my nephew George and naturally doesn't want strangers to see him being fed. But after he has eaten the singers nip in one by one to talk to him and he is the most lucid we have seen him in a while. Slowly the food turns to alcohol and alcohol to coffee, the coffee turns to coats and the coats turn to cars. And we are left alone and this is when we record the conversation I have been playing to you this evening.

**MARK: What did you think to the singers, did you enjoy them?**

**DAD:** *BUILDER'S LAMP LIGHTS UP* **They're beautiful.**

**MARK: Did you like chatting to them?**

---

* When the show returned to the Royal Opera House, the singers who performed in the bungalow performed this section of the show live with me sitting on the stool and one of them each side. Not a dry eye in the house.

DAD: *BUILDER'S LAMP LIGHTS UP* Yes.

MARK: They were very friendly weren't they?

DAD: *BUILDER'S LAMP LIGHTS UP* Yes actually they were lovely.

I said this story was about a gift. I wanted to give my dad a gift of the opera singers, the ROH singers – a gift no one else could give him and to that extent all of this is very egotistical. But I wanted to give him a feeling, an emotion, a connection. A gift you cannot commodify, a gift you can't buy and sell, a gift that flies in the face of all his political beliefs. So I am right and he is wrong. Subsequently I have turned the story of that gift into a show, sold tickets and commodified it, so he is right and I am wrong.

But there is something else. I wanted to work out why it was so important to do this concert, to have the opera, to have him back in the room for this moment. And I think it is this.

My dad and I are too old to sit down on the sofa and share. We are never going to make things right and heal old wounds and even if he wanted to my dad is no longer able. We have got to the stage where we just have to live with what we have from each other.

I wanted him back in the room so I could say the only thing left to say. I wanted to say goodbye. Because all the real goodbyes are going to be very messy and I just wanted one that was beautiful.

Funny thing is since doing the concert I don't much listen to opera now.

*EXIT WITH SACK BARROW LOADED WITH*
*GREAT COMPOSERS SERIES.*\*

---

\* My dad died on the day the performance of *Bravo Figaro!* recorded at the Royal Opera House was due for broadcast on Radio 4. My mum wanted the broadcast to go ahead. As far as I was concerned Dad died as he lived, as an inveterate heckler.

# HANNAH'S STORY

When Hannah Daykin's father injured his thumb at work five years ago, little did she realise it was the start of a devastating disease which would rob her of the dad she knew and loved.

Twenty-two-year-old Hannah was, by her own admission, a daddy's girl. Over the past five years Hannah has watched her father David change from the funny, loving and caring man she knew, into someone she barely recognises.

David, fifty-four, has the neurological condition progressive supranuclear palsy (PSP), a disease which robs people of the ability to walk, talk or communicate.

'He was a very funny dad,' recalls Hannah, from Nottingham. 'And when he wasn't funny we had to laugh at his jokes anyway!'

'I remember him taking me to my first football match when I was seven. He is a huge Nottingham Forest fan and had followed them for years. My first match we won 6–1 but I cried all the way through. I didn't like the noise.'

Today Hannah's experience of her father is very different. He is unable to walk or talk and relies on others to do everything for him.

But despite his deteriorating condition, David managed to travel from his home in Nottingham to Sheffield this summer to watch Hannah carry the Olympic Torch, to help raise awareness of PSP.

'It was an amazing experience,' said Hannah, who is studying criminology at Sheffield University. 'It was my moment of glory and I wanted to dedicate it to my dad. It was just wonderful that he made it to Sheffield to see me.'

Hannah's family first noticed changes in David after he dropped a radiator at work and tore a tendon in his arm. Looking back they now realise that accident was the first sign of the disease taking hold.

'He was off work for six weeks and after that he started acting differently,' said Hannah. 'He became obsessive about things like time. He wanted his dinner cooked at a certain time and he would insist the TV volume was always at the same level.'

The Daykins had no idea that David was becoming ill with PSP. By the time he was diagnosed in 2008 he had started to lose his balance and had fallen down the stairs on several occasions.

'He couldn't lift his head up anymore,' recalls Hannah. 'I remember being at the top of the stairs talking to him. He was at the bottom of the stairs and he couldn't look up at me.'

David's diagnosis hit the family hard as they were cata-pulted into an unknown world in which they had to adapt very quickly to rapidly changing circumstances, while at the same time come to terms with the fact they were losing their loved one.

'The diagnosis didn't feel real,' recalled Hannah. 'We didn't know what the disease was. If you are diagnosed with something like cancer people have heard it and understand it. We had to research PSP and then tell other people what it was.

'He is so different now,' she added. 'His speech is next to nothing and even though his brain will tell him not to do something his body still does it. It's heartbreaking to watch. I miss the person he was and I find it hard to see him. He's just not my dad any more.'

Hannah and her fifteen-year-old brother have been undergoing counselling to help them come to terms with the loss of their dad. Hannah has also been actively raising awareness of PSP through the media, Facebook and blogs and most recently carrying the Olympic Torch through Sheffield.

As they prepare for the future, Hannah and her family know David's death is inevitable and her mum has helped David to plan his funeral.

For Hannah, the future means working hard to ensure more people gain a better understanding of PSP, its causes and hopefully a cure.

'I know it will take a lot to find a cure. But we need to get a better understanding of PSP. That's the only way anything will change,' she added.

# WHAT IS PSP?

PSP is a degenerative brain disease which affects eye movement, balance, mobility, speech and swallowing. Over time it can rob people of the ability to walk, talk, feed themselves or communicate effectively, though they usually remain mentally alert. The average life expectancy for someone with PSP is seven years.

PSP involves the progressive death of neurons (nerve endings) in the brain. It affects people in their forties, fifties, sixties and above, the average age of onset being sixty-two. Like other neurodegenerative diseases, PSP gets worse over time.

The PSP Association is the UK's only national charity providing advice and support to people living with PSP and the related condition corticobasal degeneration (CBD), and to those who care for them.

The charity funds research into the causes of the disease, and into finding ways to develop better diagnosis and treatments. It also supports people living with PSP, their families, carers and health and social care professionals across the UK.

For more information about the PSP Association or to make a donation visit www.pspassociation.org.uk or call 01327 322410.

# CUCKOOED

# FOREWORD

When people hear about others being spied upon, be it by police or corporate infiltrators, the most common reaction is minor disbelief. There is a faint whiff of discomfort in the air, that the person talking about being spied upon is either a conspiracy theorist or a fantasist over-inflating their sense of importance and radicalism, either David Icke or Rick from *The Young Ones*.

There are variations to those reactions, a notable one being, 'Well you would be gutted if you weren't.' An assertion that implies that deep down those of us who are spied upon crave the attention to justify their sense of worth, a sort of, 'I am spied upon, therefore I am.'

My favourite reaction so far regards the Construction Blacklist, a database of workers in the construction industry who have been involved in trade union activity or voiced concerns over health and safety.

However, data was also collected about environmental and social justice activists. In 2013 the Information Commissioner's Office confirmed that my name is on the Construction Blacklist. I told a friend and he said, 'Oh that's a shame, I was going to ask you to do my patio.'

Mindful of the general disbelief and regarding the show you are about to see let me tell you this, BAE Systems (Britain's biggest arms company) have admitted to spying on Campaign

Against Arms Trade (a relatively small campaigning group with an office budget of under £250,000).*

In court documents BAE Systems not only admit to spying on CAAT they also signed a legal undertaking not to do it again.

One of the biggest arms manufacturers in the world has in effect been forced to apologise to a group of *Guardian* reading peaceniks.

Mark Thomas
July 2014

---

* BAE Systems employ 82,500 people across forty countries with sales of nearly £18bn and profits of £1.5bn. In 2010, BAE systems was fined $400 million in the US after it admitted to defrauding the USA in 'one of the largest criminal fines ever levied in the United States against a company for business related violations' and reached a £30 million settlement with the Serious Fraud Office here.

# CUCKOOED

*Onstage filings cabinets left and right facing inwards. Off centre between the cabinets a desk with an anglepoise lamp and a chair. Around the filing cabinets arch lever files, box files, leaflets, pamphlets and general activist archive debris. Back of the stage is a large projection screen. Exterior of a social club projected on screen as audience enter.*

*SFX: CARS PASSING IN SUBURBAN STREET*

*Projection changes to the interior of the social club and an audience assembling. Projection shows lights going down in club and a BAE Systems promo video\* begins playing in the club then grows to fill the whole screen as MT enters the stage.*

*MT sits down facing the projector image then as film ends turns to face audience.*

*House lights go up.*

---

\* The video shows tanks, submarines, missiles being fired and planes roaring overhead accompanied by shit generic rock music as the soundtrack. I used this footage without seeking permission from BAE Systems or paying any license fee. I figured they have had enough off of me.

# PROLOGUE

I am a very good liar, but everything I tell you in this next hour is true.

I will tell one lie and it involves the number twelve, so now you know you'll spot it.

On the 23rd May of this year I wrote a friend a letter.

*MT WALKS SR, OPENS MIDDLE DRAWER OF FILING CABINET TAKES OUT A LETTER AND READS*

Dear Martin,

Hope you and your family are well.

If you have your old mobile number you will have seen that I texted you.

I am doing a new show and it is about our relationship. It would be good to talk to you, at the very least so you can put forward your position.

It would also be good to talk because I think at some point you were my friend and I need to know what you did and didn't do with our friendship.

It doesn't have to be a recorded interview or anything

like that. It would just be good to grab a cuppa and natter. Take care

Mark

Martin was my friend for seven years. He was Campaign Co-ordinator for Campaign Against Arms Trade.

*PUTS LETTER BACK IN DRAWER\**

---

\* Someone asked me why I decided to tell this story on stage given the passage of time and that I'd written a *Guardian* article about the issue in December 2007. There are several reasons. The first was that I thought it was important to show the widespread use of police and corporate surveillance on activists. I had (and still have at the time of publication) a court case going on over the Met Police collecting information about me under the 'domestic extremist' classification and then I found out I was also on the Construction Blacklist for my political activities. I wanted to show the emotional damage of these operations, to tell a tale of love, betrayal and uncertainty. And for me, the place to set the record straight has always been on stage. It's where I feel I can be most honest and have my say.

# SCENE 1

2003.

It is a beautiful late summer morning and the sun unfolds along the Thames from the east like a golden arrow. I am outside a hotel at Tower Bridge, inside are arms dealers here for the London arms fair.*

Activists have arrived from all across the UK. We will demonstrate against the arms fair, we will protest it, march against it, hold vigils, sing, parade, blockade and lock on against it.

This is our Ascot.† Dresscode army surplus, somewhat ironically.

---

* DSEI – Defence and Security Equipment International. It's the world's largest arms fair and had its debut on the morning of 11 September 2001. As the attacks on the Twin Towers unfolded and the scale of the violence became apparent, the police appealed to the peace activists outside the arms fair to cancel their demonstration as a mark of respect for the dead and suffering. The protestors replied they would be happy to just as soon as the arms fair observed the same mark of respect and shut down for the day. It is not known if the police made this request to the arms dealers.

Two years later, at this next fair in 2003, it was reported that the organisers had to be asked if they would mind not displaying cluster bombs at the fair as it was considered 'inappropriate for the UK market', even though the UK had been using them in Iraq. Clearly it's one thing using them and another showing them off ...

† In the New York production of the show, this was changed to 'Kentucky Derby'.

8.15am. I send in two women friends in corporate black dresses, they stand in the lobby and hold up laminated signs reading,

'Complimentary bus shuttle service to the arms fair, please enquire here.'

Arms dealers start to stream across the lobby towards them.

'Free ride?'

Yes.

'Outside?'

Yes.

'When does it leave?'

Ten minutes.

'Great.'

Outside I have a hired bus now laden with arms dealers. In the planning stages one of the ideas was if the arms dealers got on the bus we should hire a Saddam Hussein impersonator to be the driver.

Beret, moustache.

'Next stop Baghdad!'

I stick with the plan that was settled on and two miles from the fair a friend stands on the front seat points a camera down the length of the bus and I get on the tannoy system.

*STANDS ON A BOX DSR*

## SFX: TO SOUND LIKE A TANNOY

'Good morning ladies and gentlemen welcome aboard the complimentary bus shuttle service to the arms fair. We are traveling at a height of about one metre off the ground and a speed of eight miles an hour, reducing to three in traffic. As members of the arms industry, you are responsible for the creation of Iraq's national debt, your companies sold weapons to Saddam Hussein,* got your governments to underwrite the deal and when Saddam defaulted on the payments, the taxpayer paid out so you were not out of pocket and then that debt gets transferred on to the Iraqi people who are still paying for the bullets of their own oppression. We know you feel very guilty, we're here to help, we're passing round a collection to help cancel Iraq's debt put as much money in as you can.'

£10.50 and an Italian arms dealer said, 'I would give you money but your tactics are Mafiosi.'

One mile away from the fair we stop.

'Ladies and gentlemen you'll have to leave now as we do not have the necessary passes to get through the police security cordon.'

'But you said you would get us to the arms fair.'

'Sorry.'

---

* Including a chemical factory – Fallujah 2. The very same factory identified by Colin Powell as a chemical weapons factory in his dossier to the UN Security Council.

'So we will have to walk about a mile?'

'Yes.'

'Past all the protestors?'

'It would appear to be the case.'

BAE Systems, Britain's biggest arms manufacturer, are not on our bus, they have their own complimentary bus, so if they will not get on our bus, we will get on theirs.

Day two. It is a beautiful late summer day and I am running in a hotel car park with Martin and Gid, Quakers, students and hippies towards the BAE Systems bus. We stand in front of it, arms raised and the bus screeches to a halt.

I duck under it and start to attach my neck to the axle of the vehicle with a bicycle D lock.

Under the bus my brain is moving faster than my body. The U of the lock goes over the axle but gets stuck on my neck and I panic and think, 'Oh fuck my neck is too fat for activism. No wonder so many of this lot are vegans. You have to be skinny for this. You never see a fat boy dangling on a Greenpeace abseil.'

*PUTS D LOCK AROUND NECK AND LOCKS IT.*
*ADDRESSES MEMBER OF AUDIENCE*

Ready to catch this? *THROWS KEY* Thanks.

I pass the key out to an activist, so I don't have the key, the police won't find it and unlock me and it buys some time.

You have to trust the person you are working with. That they will look after the key, not wander to the loo, and pass it back when you require it later.

The underside of the bus is shaded and cool, the voices outside are muffled. The chill of the concrete starts to creep into my back and the smell of oil and dust reminds me of my dad's workshop and is strangely calming.

Bobby slides in next to me.

'What are you doing, you are supposed to be doing legal observations?!?'

'I know but this looks like fun and I've brought my chain. So I'm joining in.'

Then he locks on.

ON PHONE 'Alright I've locked on, I know predictable. No, will definitely be a nick. Will miss tea. Love you.'

Compared to Bobby's calm I am a rank amateur and this is the first time I have ever been arrested. After an hour the police escort the arms dealers off the bus and tell us that the arms dealers are taking the rest of the day off because they have been traumatised.

We decide to come out.

*HOPEFULLY AUDIENCE MEMBER THROWS KEY ONSTAGE AND MT UNLOCKS D LOCK*

I come out from under the bus into the sunlight. There is a helicopter, four vans, twenty officers and a motor launch in the Thames. I am led past a crowd of onlookers to the police van – past tourists, bystanders, the curious on their way to work, the hippies and the students and pushing to the front is Martin, holding a camera,

'Oi Thommo clenched fist, photo for the paper. Clenched fist.'

I occasionally wonder what happened to that photo and if it passed over the desk of a security officer and what they saw in that picture of a man getting into a police van.

*POSES WITH A NERVOUS THUMBS UP*

In the making of this show I went and talked to friends and comrades from eleven years ago, people who knew Martin and I. Our community.

Let me introduce you.

*WALKS SL TO CABINET PULLS OPEN TOP DRAWER TO REVEAL A TELEVISION MONITOR INSIDE. IMAGE OF A HEADSHOT IS RUNNING ON IT*

This is my friend Nick Hildyard.

*PHOTO OF MT AND NH AT GLASTONBURY APPEARS BACK PROJECTOR*

Nick works at the Cornerhouse, which is an environmental and human rights NGO. He is known for being one of the most intelligent and ethical activists in the country. But for all his brilliance he is somewhat unworldly. I was once telling him about watching TV with my son and my son said,

'Dad, you are so like Homer.'

Nick said,

'Well in many ways he is right the episodic storytelling structure of you work ...'

No, we're talking about the yellow cartoon man, not the Greek fella.

*IMAGE CUTS*

*WALKS SR TO FILING CABINET PULLS OPEN TOP DRAWER TO REVEAL ANOTHER TELEVISION MONITOR INSIDE. IMAGE OF A HEADSHOT IS RUNNING ON IT*

This is Laura Nicol. She is a peace activist and Taekwondo instructor.

*PHOTO OF LN AND MT IN DRESSES LEANING ON A POLICE CAR APPEARS ON BACK PROJECTOR*

Here we are demonstrating at the US listening base in Yorkshire, Menwith Hill.* Laura is in red, I am wearing a kimono and we are sitting on a police car.

*TURNS TO SL MONITOR, IMAGE OF WOMAN APPEARS*

This is Emily Apple.†

*PHOTO OF EA WITH POLICE APPEARS ON BACK PROJECTOR*

---

* This is where I first really remember meeting Laura. Menwith Hill is nominally an RAF base but is operated and controlled by the National Security Agency, an intelligence arm of the US government, and run as an American enclave in total secrecy. It's so secret, that at the time there were no flight restrictions over it (if it doesn't exist, you can't restrict flying over it), so for a Channel 4 series we hired a hot air balloon and flew over it, narrowly avoiding crash landing in the baseball diamond on the base.

Laura and I were both demonstrating the 'Star Wars' programme at Menwith Hill, so naturally Laura turned up in full Princess Leia outfit with her boyfriend as Hans Solo. They were not the only ones; the crowd was littered with characters from the film. At one point, as the demonstration walked the sunny Yorkshire lanes around the base, some people jumped over a short wooden fence to run onto the land outside the base itself. The police promptly gave chase on quad bikes. It remains one of my favourite images of any demonstration – in the background the giant white golf-ball-like structures of the listening base and in front of them cops on quads chasing Chewbacca and Darth Vader.

† I first really remember Emily at a BAE Systems AGM when she came up and said hello. She was covered in fake blood after doing a 'die-in' during the meeting. She'd been thrown out. I remember thinking at the time the great irony in the anti-arms movement was that without army surplus half of them would be naked.

She was a direct action queen as this photo attests.

*ADDRESSES SL MONITOR*

Emily, I always had you as being close with Martin

**EMILY:** *LISTENS* **Yeah we were. He was a really, really, really good friend.**

To the extent that your son, well, Martin was his godfather.

**EMILY: Secular godfather, yeah.**

That's Emily.

*MAN'S FACE APPEARS ON SR MONITOR*

This is Gid Burrows* and in a previous incarnation protesting the arms trade.

*PHOTO OF GB COVERED IN BLOOD ON DEMO APPEARS ON BACK PROJECTOR*

Gid was in his early twenties when he met Martin, who was something of a father figure to him, though not necessarily a traditional one.

---

\* I met Gid at a CAAT benefit gig he was compering. I used to do a fair few of them in the Union Chapel in Islington and the Hackney Empire and I was perhaps less tolerant of the Quaker contingent than I am now. On stage, I said the lovely thing about working with Quakers is that if they piss you off, you can punch them and they won't hit you back. One night someone shouted at me over this line and I used the old Bill Hicks line, 'You're a Christian, forgive me.' To the audience's delight he shouted back, 'We do, Mark, we do.'

**GID: I was dancing on the table with that bloke in a club in Wolverhampton totally pissed out of our heads.**

Gid like Emily, Laura and I were close to him, we hung out together. He stayed with us, we stayed with him. I shared a bed with him.

**GID: *INTERRUPTS* I saw him naked over thirty times.**

Gid has a tendency to over-share.

These people are going to help tell the story.

The police arresting suite is a long high desk, dotted with computers and police officers.

'Name? address? Keys, phone. Occupation?'

'Comedian.'

Cop at the end says,

'On a fucking good night he is.'

I have just been heckled by a cop and my comeback is cutting and vicious and I think of it on the way home.

In the cell it is cooler than outside, it is tiled, bed of wood and it is dull. Whenever activists tell me they are doing something that may end in their arrest I always say, 'take a book'.

After a long time a police officer enters the cell.

'Mr Thomas, we have a solicitor on the phone for you.'

'I have spoken to one already.'

'Well there is another sir, wants to check we have not abused your human rights. This way, sir. Use the phone on the wall.'

'Hello ...'

A voice the other end says,

'Ahhh, you wanker.' It's Martin. He has blagged his way through the switchboard pretending to be a lawyer.

'Got anything to read?'

'No.'

'I'll see if I can get them to take a copy of *Razzle* at the front desk.'

'No, don't!'

'I'll tell them if you don't have a wank every two hours you get violent.'

I reckon they knew he was not a lawyer as I giggled all the way back to the cell.

Later that evening I am charged with criminal damage, later still there is a two-day trial where I am acquitted on the grounds that they could not find any criminal damage and it is still entirely possible to be found innocent in the British courts if they can find no evidence of a crime having occurred.*

---

* The same can't be said of the police officer who handled my case, Detective Sergeant Richard de Cadenet who, as it turns out, used a Met Police office credit card to pay for his holidays in Thailand and Mexico, racked up over £70,000 of personal spending and was subsequently jailed for ten months for fraud.

I go to leave the station. I am not a hero. I am an everyman, like you, an ordinary person. I do not expect a mob, banners with my name and cheering, I do not expect my face merged with the iconic Che Guevara image on a t-shirt, I do not expect children to be named after me, to be showered in flowers and songs written in my name. But a small group and a pat on the back would be nice.

No one.

There is no one. Except Martin.

Deck shoes, chinos, golf shirt, wire glasses, ruddy face, his hair swept back.

'Come on, mate – let's get a drink!'

# SCENE 2

Ours was a friendship born in protest.

I ask Emily, 'What demos did you go on with Martin?'

*EA APPEARS ON SL MONITOR*

**EMILY: We went on a lot of the May Day protests together, we went to Genoa together, the G8 protests there, we got teargassed together there, we went to New York together.**

Do you think when you get teargassed with someone, this sounds weird, but when you get teargassed with someone, do you think that is a binding experience?

**EMILY: I think a lot of activism is, whenever you do those sort of things where you are in a highly charged, adrenalin-fuelled situation and you are quite often doing something quite dangerous the bonds you get with people are immense.**

Eleven years later and we are quick to find fondness in our memories of him.

*LN APPEARS SR MONITOR*

Laura, describe Martin for these people.

LAURA: Describe him? Cockney builder.

EMILY: One of the things I always loved about him was that he was so different and he didn't give a shit about being different.

Gid, what was Martin like with other activists?

*GB APPEARS SR MONITOR*

GID: Totally inappropriate and brutally honest.

*EA APPEARS SL MONITOR*

Emily, describe to the audience Martin's sense of humour?

EMILY: *LISTENS* Dry, dirty and sarcastic and that's what I love ...

CAAT was founded by Quakers in the 1970s and they have never been able to shake that image. In truth they are mainly *Guardian* reading atheists, either way neither Quakers nor the *Guardian* reading atheists are noted for their Monday mornings stories of weekend excess. Quaker stories go:

'How was your weekend?'

'I went on a retreat.'

'How was it?'

'Quiet.'

Martin walks in Monday,

'Bloody hell. My missus found the Viagra in my coat pocket. "Who you fucking, you seeing someone else?" "No, no it's for you, I'm getting on a bit and I wanted to look after you." "Alright I believe you and you're on for tonight." So that night she goes upstairs, I pop a Viagra and wait ten minutes, I go upstairs and she is asleep. I wake her up. "I thought we were on?" "Sorry love I'm tired, we'll do it tomorrow." So I had to go and watch the fucking football, sitting on the sofa with a cup of tea and a raging hard on for three hours.'

The Quakers couldn't really relate to that.

As someone who stood outside of our immediate group, Nick, how would you assess him?

*NH APPEARS SL MONITOR*

**NICK:** *LISTENS* **There was everything in Martin that was totally dedicated to the cause, an anti arms trade campaigner, but not only anti arms trade but a campaigner who was interested in other issues, who saw the value in being able to link campaigns, I mean he wasn't only a foot soldier.**

I ran a campaign with Nick about dam building in the Kurdish region of Turkey – fairly esoteric even by our standards but Martin was all over it. He was interested in pro-democracy, internationalist and anti-capitalist campaigns. I called him one morning, I forget what for.

'I can't talk, I'm chained to a petrol pump.'

'What?'

'Friends of the Earth, climate change, funding Bush, blood for oil.'

'Are there cops there?'

'The cops came over and said how long are you going to be here? I said I don't know. They said well let us know when you have finished.'

'You're kidding?'

'I know, they could have had me for trespass but if they weren't going to say anything, I wasn't. They did get a bit narky when I had a fag.'

One time, we were at a Green Party auction and there was a room with all the things you could bid for laid out – gift certificates for Reiki healing, driftwood that looks like Gandhi and a biodegradable bamboo death pod.* There was a big picture up for auction, of the Iraq anti-war march in London, taken from way back and high up. You can see thousands and thousands of people wandering the streets, tiny dots and Martin says,

'Fuck me, that's me!'

And it was.

His character was so much larger than life that he stood out in a march of millions.

These were my friends. Authentic, genuine activists.

---

* This is absolutely true. The Green Party did indeed have a bamboo sarcophagus in the auction and there was some confusion over who had actually made the winning bid and was rightful owner of the death pod.

And Martin he ticked every box I had, working class, rough as shit, prone to kindness, easy to shed a tear, he used to work for the arms industry* and had now redeemed himself and now worked against.† He ticked every box in every Johnny Cash song I have ever loved.

Three weeks later Martin is accused of being a spy for Britain's biggest arms company. BAE Systems.

He has always publicly denied it.

At the time I was working in television, not an industry noted for its authenticity, and the programmes I made did involve an element of deception. It would be unfair to suggest I liked the deception, it would not be correct to say I liked deceiving people. I loved it.

In one particular show I set up a PR company, Mackintosh Morley and hired a stall at an arms fair in Greece, offering PR advice on how to handle allegations of human rights abuse.‡

---

* He told us he used to work for the South African arms manufacturer, Denel.
† Martin started as a volunteer at CAAT in 1997, eventually becoming the paid Campaign Co-ordinator from 2000–03.
‡ It's up on the internet somewhere. If you can find it, you can enjoy the whole thing. In that series of shows we got a credible admission of torture and the Defence Attaché to London, Colonel Halim Nawi, admitted Indonesia was using British supplied equipment in East Timor, which contravened official UK policy that weapons sold would not be used for 'internal oppression or external aggression' and questions were asked in parliament about it. (28 Jan 1999, Column 480, House of Commons Debate, *Hansard*)

The company was the first stall people saw on the official tour. So ministers and generals would walk past and see a massive poster with the words,

'ARE YOU READY WHEN AMNESTY INTER-NATIONAL COME KNOCKING AT YOUR DOOR?'

Lots of military people stopped and said,

'You are Amnesty International?'

'No we're not. But we could be. We are the people who will help you when they do come for you, we are the people who will teach you how to handle yourself against human rights allegations. We're running free media training courses; takes five minutes, come on in.'

Day two. We stand sipping coffee first thing as a man in a jacket and tie arrives.

'My name is Major General Widjojo, I am from the Indonesian armed forces, I wish to try your media training session.'

'Come on in.'

*MT MOVES CHAIR DSL FACING TABLE AND TWISTS ANGLEPOISE LAMP TO SHINE ON CHAIR*

'This is Chris, he'll be interviewing you. Simon is going to film it so we can do an in-depth assessment of your media skills and as Chris interviews you, I'm going to offer you advice and tactics. Now to take the sting out of the criticism I am going to give you some toys – soldiers, animals and superheroes. If you answer well I shall give you more, if you answer badly I shall take them away. OK? Off we go.'

Chris opens a large file containing Amnesty reports and begins.

'Major General Widjojo you are accused of genocide in East Timor ...'

Major General Widjojo interrupts,

'Amnesty International do not understand the situation. They are a Western organisation. They simply do not understand cultural differences ...'

'Uh oh oh that's quite an aggressive answer, I am going to have to take away an octopus and Spiderman ... We work on a policy of partial admission. Can you admit to any of the accusations? Only do it if it is true, only do it if you feel you can, but can you admit to some of them?'

'Yes. I can admit to torture.'

'Torture?'

'Just a little bit of torture.'

'Just a little bit. Yes let's start with a little bit and see if you can win Spiderman back.'

Major General Widjojo looks at the camera and looks at me and says,

'This isn't going anywhere is it?'

'No I promise, this is just between you and me.'

## *CLIP FROM MAJOR GENERAL INTERVIEW PLAYS ON BACK PROJECTOR*

It transpires that Martin and I shared a talent for deception and fair play to him he did it for seven years. But deception is a heady drug and you have to control the usage.

Before I went to the arms fair I spoke to the Channel 4 lawyers, a chap called Neil Pepin.*

'Right so you want to film undercover, well there are regulations.'

'Yes.'

'You have to catch them do something illegal, lying or something that is against the public interest. Those are the rules – illegal, lying, against the public interest. Do you think anyone at the arms fair might fall into those categories?'

'We might get lucky.'

'And you have to reveal the deception as soon as possible, put the allegations you are going to make about the arms dealers to them and broadcast their right of reply.'

---

* Hunter S Thompson once wrote, 'The TV business is uglier than most things. It is normally perceived as some kind of cruel and shallow money trench through the heart of the journalism industry, a long plastic hallway where thieves and pimps run free and good men die like dogs, for no good reason.' I've always liked that quote, but fifteen years after stopping work with Channel 4, I still keep in contact with Neil Pepin.

I liked the deception, I liked the regulations, I liked that you reveal the deception afterwards, because I am a show off and it is pointless doing this if I can't brag about it.

# SCENE 3

*WOMAN APPEARS SL MONITOR*

Let me introduce you to one more person. This is Ann Feltham.

*PHOTO OF ANN ON BACK PROJECTOR*

She is Parliamentary Co-ordinator for Campaign Against Arms Trade.* I say she runs CAAT – no one on the left runs anything. If you say who's in charge they say, 'We have a horizontal consensual decision making process.'

It's the 26th September 2003.

**ANN: It was a Friday afternoon.**

*FRAME FREEZES*

Ann is in the office when there's a knock on the door

**ANN: It was a *Sunday Times*' journalist and he had one sheet of paper with a kind of report he said had gone to BAE that was describing activities that were going on in our office ...**

---

\* Ann has worked at CAAT since 1985.

## FRAME FREEZES

If I may, Ann has just met a journalist from the *Sunday Times'* Insight team, their investigative team, and they are about to run one of their biggest scoops of the year. Anne goes with him to the *Sunday Times* office.

ANN: ... where they showed us this heap of papers which were kind of X went to a meeting and Y went to a meeting and all sorts of details about what had been going on in our office.

## LIGHT COMES UP ON REPORT ON DESK

It revealed that a man called Alan Fossey had been spying on CAAT in Hull.

ANN: It was quite apparent that some other people had been spying on us as well.

Did they say or suggest who it might be?

ANN: They didn't suggest who it might be.

Ann goes back to the office, runs an audit of the office computers and produces a file of evidence.

## NH APPEARS ON SL MONITOR

NICK: Ann gave me the file and I sat down in the top room at CAAT in their old offices and I read it and it was extremely forensic and having read it there was absolutely no doubt in my mind that it was Martin.

*MT ON PHONE*

Get Ann out of the meeting, I want to speak to Ann, get Ann on the phone. I'd love to leave a message. What are you doing attacking the most productive and active member of CAAT? You have just vilified the one person in CAAT who actually does anything. He campaigns, he gets out there. If BAE are paying him, they should give him a pay rise, cos he does more work than anyone else. What is it you actually do? Other than look smug. Gone on a vigil. Did you light a candle for peace, did you and the nuns sing a song against the arms industry? It is amazing the arms industry still functions after you have given them one of your sincere looks. Why don't you just fuck off, fuck off with your smug arrogant middle-class *Guardian* Quaker twattery AND YOUR PORRDIGE IS SHIT TOO.

I must have been quite a handful that day.

*ANN APPEARS SL MONITOR*

Ann, that couldn't have been very nice for whoever picked up the phone.

**ANN: Yeah.**

I'm sorry about that.

*ANN LOOKS ON IN SILENCE*

Ann doesn't accept my apology. It was just that all of this was incomprehensible to us.

*LN APPEARS SR MONITOR*

Laura, when Martin was accused of spying on CAAT what was your reaction?

LAURA: *LISTENING* I didn't believe it.

Why didn't you?

LAURA: The things he'd been involved in it didn't seem possible and also I don't think it was helped by the fact the people accusing him didn't like him.

What do you mean, the things he'd done?

LAURA: The things he'd been involved in. I mean he'd pied Dick Evans, hadn't he?

Dick Evans?

LAURA: He'd pied Dick Evans.

Dick Evans was the Chairman of BAE Systems! Martin stuck a custard pie in his face.

*GB APPEARS SR MONITOR*

Gid, do you remember when Martin pied Dick Evans?

GID: *LISTENS* I was sitting next to him.

He was making a speech to some students at some London business school ...

GID: And we just decided we'd get in there and custard pie him, use spray cream or shaving cream, because you can get them into anywhere, and straight into the face.

Naïvely, stupidly, inanely we thought he can't be a spy – he put a custard pie in Dick Evans' face.

But more than this, this is our friend.

To even look at the file would be an act of betrayal.

What did I do when I found out my friend had been accused of spying? I took him on tour.

# SCENE 4

*SFX: LOUD DUB MUSIC PLAYING. MT V.O. AND MUSIC DIPS JUST BELOW HIS SHOUTED VOICE*

Four of us in the car, Bobster is tour manager.

He did the shortest tour manager's job interview ever. I said,

'Who else have you worked with?'

He said,

'The first job I had was doing lights for the Clash.'

In the back seat is Sam a crustie of indeterminate origin, he looks like a Womble* with a hard on and a can of Tennent's.†

Sitting next to him is Martin, smoking cheap fags and moaning about the loud dub Sam insists on playing. Every now and again Sam thinks he is part of the sound system and will shout from nowhere, 'Rewind Selector' which is

---

* I discovered when performing this in New York that Womble doesn't translate. Despite Great Uncle Bulgaria's alleged global wanderings they remain unknown, so we changed the image to Animal from *The Muppets*.

† Tennent's doesn't translate either, but I can't remember what we used instead – maybe a six pack.

really annoying. We are driving in the narrow country lanes on the Yorkshire moors. Bobby is driving fast, the music is loud, outside the dry stone walls speed past and the sunlight flashes between the shadows of the hedgerows into the car – bright and shade, bright and shade, bright and shade.

'Oi! There is a stone circle near here, pull over pull over.'

We pull over and leave Bobster in the car and Sam and Martin and I head off for the stone circle.*

*SFX: MUSIC FADES DOWN*

I can't remember if we found the stone circle but I do remember the shape of the hills and the way the land slides across the skyline, the dips and folds of the earth, ridges and steps of collapsed soil. I remember the grass and the dark peaty brown earth and the pools of water collecting in hollows. And I remember Martin going, 'Fucking hell look what I've found!' and holding up a ram's skull† replete with horns.

We show it to Bobster and he says,

---

\* I have a love of stone circles. I hasten to add that this is nothing to do with paganism, spirituality or religion. I just like them, they are often in beautiful places and they are part of my roots and culture.

† I took the skull home, cleaned it and placed it alongside a couple of others I had in the children's bathroom. As is the nature of stuff like this, it didn't last too long and so we had to source a new skull for the show from a junk shop and held it together with resin for the tour.

'Chain it to the radiator grill of the Jag, fuck it. It's a hire car.'

We tie the skull to the car, open the doors, turn the music up and pose for photos.

'Oi! Oi! Oi! Oi!'

'In the area!'

'Come on!'

*SFX: MUSIC CUTS*

Martin spends half the time with me on tour and the other half working at Leeds Castle in Kent.

'What you doing there?'

'Cleaning out the gutters.'

'How much do they pay you?'

'£50 a day ... two ducks and a pheasant. They don't know about the ducks and the pheasant.'

Nick kept telling me I should see the file, 'if only for your own peace of mind.'

And I am not at peace. Martin's behaviour is sometimes awkward, defensive, and there are only a handful of us left who believe in him. But in truth it is the fear of betrayal, an unwillingness to consider deception, that rushes in to fill the space where loyalty once lay.

*GB APPEARS SR MONITOR*

GID: At the end when it was just you me and Emily defending him, it was fair to say we were pretty much deluded. Or we were allowing him to delude us.

# SCENE 5

Now at this stage you may be asking yourselves a question. 'Why would a multi-million pound, transnational corporation like BAE spy on a group of Quakers and *Guardian* readers?'

Now let's be honest about this, it is the Festival,* some of you have seen five shows already today, it's warm and some of you have glazed over already. I am not judging, it's just that I can see more of you than you think I can. Now this answer involves some facts and figures and frankly some of you are not going to make it over the hump.

So for those of you who are glazing over, here's 'The Girl from Ipanema'.

*SFX: MUSIC PLAYS*

Just regard it as being put on hold and we'll be back in a minute.

For the rest of you, 1975 – Indonesia invades East Timor and kills one third of the population. BAE† have a rolling contract to supply fighter jets to Indonesia.

---

* Edinburgh, where this was first performed in 2014. During the tour, I'd replace this with wherever we were and whatever venue it was.
† The company became BAE Systems in 1999 after a merger with Marconi.

In 1996, a group of women decide to break into BAE hangers in Lancashire. They find the jets that are destined for Indonesia, identifying the flags and serial number and smash up the cockpit with hammers. They then phone security to hand themselves in.

Four were arrested* and put on remand, charged with conspiracy and criminal damage. In court the judge allows them to run a defence that says it is legal in English law to commit a small crime in order to prevent a greater crime from occurring, i.e. it is legal to break a plane in order to stop the plane killing civilians.

BAE are put in the dock. Witnesses are called from East Timor and human rights monitors testify.

The jury acquit the women.

BAE have the ignominy of having had £1.5 million worth of damage done to their state-of-the-art fighter plane, which ironically is not hammer proof, they then end up on trial, lose in the court of public opinion and the jury let the activists walk free.

And it is at this point that BAE decides to put Campaign Against Arms Trade on the radar.

OK 'The Girl from Ipanema' people ... CLAPS ... back in the room.

Nick kept saying see the file.

---

* Angie Zelter, Joanna Wilson, Lotta Kronlid and Andrea Needham – the Ploughshare 4.

*ANN APPEARS SL MONITOR*

Ann, I remember phoning you and asking whether I could look at the file.

**ANN:** *LISTENS* **After you'd spoken to Nick.**

Yeah, I had spoken with Nick and he'd always said I should check out the file.

**ANN: Yeah.**

It was something else, Ann, that made me phone you too, not quite sure what. Were you surprised when I phoned you?

**ANN: I was pleased, I always thought that the people closest to it needed to read it.**

The CAAT office in north London is an old Georgian building. The staircases are long, narrow and dark. I touch the side of the wall, walking them and at the top, the very top floor is a box room, a couple of filing cabinets and a table, used for meetings and storage. On the table is the file.

I feel sick but I feel ready.

*BLACKOUT SAVE ANGLEPOISE ON DESK*

The main evidence against Martin.

The internal audit of CAAT's computers reveal that Martin had been forwarding internal emails to a third party.

Hundreds and hundreds of them, year after year.

The email is linked to a company run by a woman called Evelyn Le Chene.

*COMPANIES HOUSE DOCUMENTS FOR EVELYN*
*LE CHENE PROJECTED ONTO MAIN SCREEN*

Her company is called Threat Response Initiative. These are her company documents. She runs a spy company, collecting information on CND members, CAAT, trade unions and leftists. A company would pay a joining fee then you paid for information on an individual basis. You could get an individual's name, address, phone number, NI number, known associates and political affiliations. And it cost £2.25 per person.

£2.25.

In court documents BAE Systems admit to spying on Campaign Against Arms Trade.

*LEGAL CONSENT ORDER PROJECTED ONTO*
*MAIN SCREEN*

And admit to hiring Evelyn Le Chene ...

*LEGAL CONSENT ORDER HIGHLIGHTING*
*LE CHENE NAME PROJECTED ONTO MAIN*
*SCREEN.*

... to spy on Campaign Against Arms Trade. The directors of Threat Response Initiative are interesting.

*COMPANIES HOUSE DOCUMENTS FOR BARRIE*
*GANE PROJECTED ONTO MAIN SCREEN*

One is Barrie Charles Gane CMG, OBE – Barry Charles Gane CMG OBE – who is ex-deputy director of MI6.

To send email to the wrong address is commonplace, everyone in this room has done it, bar those still sending pigeons.

To send hundreds of emails to the wrong address is clumsy.

To send hundreds of emails by mistake to Threat Response Initiative ... that's un-fucking-believable!

I phone my friends.

*MONTAGE PROJECTED ONTO MAIN SCREEN*

EMILY: The absolute fucking betrayal.

LAURA: Complete betrayal of trust.

NICK: It was a shattering revelation for you.

ANN: I did think there had been betrayal but I had never been the closest to him.

GID: I asked him is there anything you want to say and he said there was no truth in it whatsoever. And a good friend would not have done that, a good friend would have said, OK, its over ... And I can't, I can't come to terms with that.

This may sound incongruous but I think the phrase I am looking for is 'revenge fuck'. What do you do when you get fucked over by an arms company? You fuck over an arms company back.

First of all you set up an arms company – it is easy to set one up.

*ADDRESSING AUDIENCE*
Can you give me the name of an English county?

*ADDRESSING AUDIENCE*
You, an item a Norman or Viking might have.

*USES FIRST AND SECOND ANSWER*
... is the name of our arms company.

*ADDRESSING AUDIENCE*
Can I ask the name of your first pet?

*ADDRESSING AUDIENCE*
Can you tell me your grandmother's surname?

Right, the CEO of our company is Major General *USES LAST TWO ANSWERS*

Now we need a couple of mobile phones, one from overseas to make you international, some email addresses and a hot desk at a shared office, with a secretary who says, 'I'm afraid he is not in. I will pass on your number and he will call as soon as possible.'

Now you can talk to arms dealers.

If I phone an arms company and say, 'Hi I'm working at the Traverse Theatre* and ...'

*SFX: PHONE GOING DEAD*

If I phone up and say,

---

* Obviously this changed from venue to venue during the tour, otherwise it wouldn't have been accurate.

'Hi it's *INSERTS NAME OF COMPANY AND CEO* we're an arms company and want to buy guns.'

They say,

'Of course you are, why would you call us otherwise, what kind of guns would you like?'

'Big ones.'

'Would you like bullets?'

'Yes please.'

'Can I supersize you with a mortar round?'

'Would you mind?'

If arms dealer talks to you they will explain what they are willing to do.

First one is a South London* arms dealer offering to sell illegal electroshock torture equipment. But it wasn't enough that he agreed to supply them, I asked,

'Would you supply them to Zimbabwe and break UN sanctions?'

'Yes'

I call HMRC and he is shut down.

Next, DSEi, the London arms fair. I find four companies selling illegal torture equipment. The *Guardian* runs with the story in enough time to see three of them kicked out of the fair.

---

* Tony Lee, TLT International.

Three, I find a dealer discharging an electroshock baton in the middle of a police and security fair in Birmingham. He stands there with the blue flashes and the electric cackle, cops are walking past not one of them seeming to realise that possession, advertising and discharging an electroshock baton is illegal.

I try and find a cop to arrest the guy, it is harder than you might think.

First cop says, 'I'm off duty.'

Second says 'I know you, you're Mark Thomas, I like your programmes but I don't want to be in them, fuck off.'

Third one is standing at the end of an aisle, full uniform and hi vis, he is a cardboard cut-out for Poundland.

It is impossible to find a cop at the police fair. I go to the organisers' office and explain what is happening. The guy is arrested, he does four months in jail and is deported.

Next, I stop one of the UK's largest arms companies exporting military equipment to Sudan.

Next I get asked to provide evidence for the House of Commons' Select Committee,* I write two reports and am asked to give oral evidence. I sit before the Committee and I blame HMRC for not enforcing the laws and doing

---

* I was asked by Roger Berry, the Chair. You can find the report here: www.publications.parliament.uk/pa/cm200506/cmselect/cmquad/873/87302.htm#evidence. The committee commended my actions and I sent Roger Berry a note saying if a group of MPs ever commends me again, I'll take legal action.

the simple work I have done. HMRC get called before the Committee. HMRC are extremely pissed off.

Two weeks later I get a VAT inspection.

As revenge fucks go it's not bad – doesn't deal with the emotional turmoil but it did reclaim my dignity as an activist, it did make me feel better about myself and I was down to a size 12.

Twelve.

2007, three years since I last saw Martin I get off the train and walk to his house, rehearsing the questions I want to ask. He lives in a two-up two-down, there is no fence for the garden. He isn't in but his wife answers the door and I know her and she instinctively says,

'Oh come in Thommo, come in.'

She ushers me in to the hall and says,

'I can't say anything, I daren't say anything.'

It has no wallpaper and a plastic laundry basket in the corner and we go into the living room and she repeats that she can't say anything and that Martin has been depressed and he has lost all his friends. And I say I wish we were meeting under other circumstances and leave.

If Martin was working for BAE Systems he doesn't seem to have been well paid. And it is odd that I am worried about a traitor's terms and conditions. BAE Systems still expands in the financial military sphere and Evelyn Le Chene was voted president of the Rotary club, so accepted into, well not polite society but nearly. And it is hard to know who the villain is when there are no regulations controlling these companies and people who do this work. Not one law. Not even a register.

I found out where Evelyn Le Chene lives. I have her home address.

*ADDRESSES AUDIENCE*

Who would like to know where she lives?

This is a show about data theft, get a grip on yourself!

I write her a letter.

Dear Evelyn Le Chen,

You once collected data about me and I wondered if I could ask for like for like in return.

Did you employ Martin to spy on CAAT and myself?

How much did you pay him?

What data did he collect about me?

Hope you can help, I have enclosed £2.25 for your troubles.

I write the same letter to Barrie Gane,

Except I add the line,

'As an ex-deputy director of MI6 you are probably wondering how I got your address ...'

On the 23rd May I write to Martin asking him to talk to me.

Dear Martin, if you have your old mobile number you will have seen I texted you a while back. I am doing a show and it is about our relationship.

I want him to admit it what he has done. I want to know who paid him?

How much they paid him? How was he paid?

How was he recruited? When they recruited him? What was his remit?

How did he pass on information? What information?

About who? To whom?

Who else was involved?

What data of mine was passed on? Who saw it?

Why did they want it? Where is it now?

But most of all I want him to confess.

He sent me a letter back, undated,

'I think to open, old, deep and still unhealed wounds can only be a negative.'

7th July 2014. It's a beautiful early summer morning and the sun shines down the River Medway. I am running in a car park with a cameraman behind me, running towards Martin.

*SLOW MOTION FOOTAGE ON MAIN PROJECTOR SCREEN OF MT APPROACHING MAN IN CAR PARK. MAN'S FACE IS DELIBERATELY BLURRED*

Martin backs away from me, he is shorter than I remembered him, fatter and greyer too. He is still smoking and I
recognise his smell.

He says,

'What's the camera for?'

I say,

'It's to record the event.'

He has noticed the camera, this is not covert filming and I
tick a regulation box.

I say,

'You need to talk to us mate, you need to admit what you
have done.'

He says, 'What does it matter one way or the other now?'

*FILM CUTS*

I made a decision not to show you Martin's face, not to
mention his surname within these walls, not to mention his
family's names, nor play you his voice, not to show or tell
you where he lives.

So how do you know that what I'm about to tell you is true?
Trust. I ask you to trust me.

Martin says,

'You don't know the damage this has done to me. How this
has affected my personal and family life. There is not a day
goes by when I don't think of you and Em, Gid, Laura. You

were my best friends and I loved what we did together. I look back on that as the golden years of my life. Do you think I could do the things I did without believing it?'

I say,

'That is not the issue. Will you admit to what you have done? You owe us, when everyone else left you we stayed. We defended you for a year. You owe us.'

## FILM PLAYS AGAIN – MARTIN AND MT HUG

'I will talk to you, not now, let me sort things out.'

He says, 'I will talk to you.'

We hug.

He has a Unite bag.

He is the trade union rep here.

## FILM SHOWS SECURITY MEN STOPPING FILMING

It is a beautiful early summer's day and we are driving back to London. I am on the ceiling. Full of adrenaline, caffeine, hope, trust, logic, friendship, disbelief, optimism, shock, memories good and bad, happiness.

The phone goes and it is Martin,

'Thommo, sorry mate but your presence this morning has triggered a security alert and the police are here with me and want to contact you and I am phoning to ask is it OK for me to give them your telephone number?'

BUT he will talk. I am running for the tube, still full of caffeine and adrenaline down the steps at Kings Cross, hoodie up, thermos of coffee from the stake out 'cos we have been up since four in the morning. Still full of confusion, hope and elation, I dash for the tube and I bump into Hillary Benn and Ed Miliband.

Hillary says,

'Hello Mark.'

Ed Miliband says,

'Mark Thomas, what have you been up to?'

'I have been staking out a corporate spy who has been infiltrating the democratic protest groups and you should have an investigation not just into him but a full public enquiry into blacklisting, undercover cops ...'

'We are going to have an inquiry.'

'But not a public one, it needs to be public.'

And I bend his ear from Kings Cross to Green Park and I step back and see myself hoodie up, wide-eyed, ranting and waving a thermos into the face of the Leader of the Opposition.*

On the 9th July two days later I receive this text from Martin:

---

* Some time after the show started to tour, I bumped into Hillary Benn at Oxford station. 'Friends of mine tell me I'm in the show,' he said, 'I remember bumping into you on the tube.' The look he gave me indicated that I must have come across as fairly wired at the time.

## *TEXT APPEARS ON MAIN PROJECTOR*

I have carefully and with much soul searching considered
your proposal to meet and talk I can not see any personal
positives in re opening the whole issue. I therefore with
respect decline to meet and would ask you please to cease
with what is risking becoming intrusive. I hope your shows
go well and wish you well for the future.

Emily says, 'It is Martin keeping his last bit of power by not telling us. So we have to keep going back to him.'

Gideon says, 'Mark, that's twice you've held the door open for him and twice he's walked away. Perhaps it's time you did the same.'

Laura says, 'Ah, fuck him!'

For forty-eight hours I was filled with mindless optimism and hope, that he would do the right thing. Forty-eight hours of deluded yearning, that he would tell the truth and for the first time in seventeen years he could have acted like a friend, that he would be a good guy. Because when you tell the truth you're no longer a bad guy, you're a whistle blower.

## *SHUTS CABINET DRAWERS SL AND SR AND TURNS OFF LAMP*

You remember the picture of the club at the beginning of the show?

You remember the people arriving to watch the show?

Well I hired a club to put on a secret preview of this show. I bussed people in to see it. They didn't know where they were going, and those who were driving were sworn to secrecy. The club I hired was the BAE Systems Sports and Social Club in Rochester. The audience were friends and activists some of whom I have known since I was eleven. My community gathered on BAE land to hear this story, to hear our story because nearly half of the people in that audience had been spied upon by police or corporate interests. Afterwards amidst hugs and spilt drinks and moaning about 'the chips you promised', I ask some of those people to come and sit in this chair and I said to them, tell them who you are.

## FILM PLAYS ON MAIN PROJECTOR

DAVE SMITH: My name is Dave Smith and I am a black-listed construction worker. My name is on a secret list that all the big companies did and every time I went for a job when I went for the site induction on site I used to give them my national insurance number. By the end of the induction when everyone else got taken on I never got the job and it happened time and time again and I was just out of work all the time during the time of a massive building boom and it's not just me there are 3,200 of us on this file.

LOIS AUSTEN: I was the National Chair of Youth Against Racism in Europe and I was spied on by Peter Francis who also spied on the Lawrence family. The reason for him spying on me, apparently, was so that a Special Branch file could be compiled on the anti-racist campaign activity I was involved in.

GUY TAYLOR: I'm Guy Taylor, I work for Globalise Resistance and we found out our police spy when he left a message on someone's answer machine when he was grassing people up to the cops. We kicked him out.

SURESH GROVER: My name is Suresh Grover I am a civil rights activist and I campaign with families who have suffered racial violence and miscarriages of justice. I know I have been spied on because I made families hold the police and state authorities to account.

MARK: Who spied on you?

SURESH GROVER: SDS, Special Branch, MI5.

'ALISON': I am known as Alison and I had a five year relationship with undercover police officer Mark Jenner who I knew as Mark Cassady and whom I loved very much.

JASON PARKINSON: I'm Jason Parkinson. I am a freelance video journalist and I have ended up on the domestic extremist database and I have been tracked since February 2006 for doing my job.

*CLIPS OF OTHERS FLASH UP*

*'One of my best friends for seven years was an undercover police officer we now know as Mark Kennedy.'*

*'I was spied on by Mark Jenner.'*

*'I was spied upon because I was an anti-racist activist.'*

*'Two unnamed officer tried to recruit me as a mole.'*

*'Two of them turned out to be spies.'*

*'I have been under surveillance since 1996 and have been on the domestic extremist database since 2000.'*

So here is the question, at what point do we say enough?

After an old liberal gets duped?

After 3,200 blacklisted workers are illegally denied employment?

After undercover cops deceive women into relationships with them?

After families see their children murdered and campaign for justice only to find those charged with finding them justice are spying on them?

Surely when we hear that the Stephen Lawrence family was spied on all of us have to say

'Enough', don't we?

*BLACKOUT**

---

* Throughout the show, I refer to the Quakers with some degree of scorn. However, it is more often than not that I encounter Quakers on direct action and protests against the arms industry. I may not have any faith but to those that use their faith to give them courage to defy an inhuman world, SALUT!
  And if I ever turn religious I'm going to be a Quaker.
  A really, really noisy Quaker.

# ANN'S STORY

This was the second time we had been told arms company BAE Systems was spying on us. In September 2003 a *Sunday Times* journalist turned up in the Campaign Against Arms Trade office to tell us of infiltration organised by Evelyn Le Chene. Now, in January 2007, we learned through a phone call from our solicitor that we'd been spied on again.

The previous month Tony Blair had stopped the Serious Fraud Office's investigation of BAE's deals with Saudi Arabia. CAAT, together with social justice organisation The Corner House, was mounting a legal challenge to this. During the Christmas break I had sent an email containing our lawyer's advice on the legal action to the members of CAAT's Steering Committee. That email had ended up with BAE. Its lawyers, under a solicitors' ethical code, had to tell CAAT's lawyers, hence that January phone call.

Our lawyers had to go to court to force BAE to reveal its source. It was a Paul Mercer.

Then it was back to court to get him to say how he had got hold of the email. Over the following months the story dripped out. BAE had quite a few of our emails. In November 2007 BAE finally admitted paying both Mrs Le Chene and Paul Mercer, and promised not to spy on CAAT again.

The second spying episode was not as traumatic as the first. In 2003 it had been devastating to find that Martin was among the eight or so people Mrs Le Chene had infiltrated into CAAT. Even for those of us who had not become a very close friend, he had still been a valued colleague. For six years we had enjoyed his involvement and company.

We did not know Paul Mercer so this made 2007 a less painful experience. However, there were some similarities. On both occasions our legal advice was that very few people should be told what was happening while investigations took place and lawyers exchanged letters. CAAT is usually an open organisation so this caused problems both within the staff and committees, and with the wider campaigning community. Although this secrecy is probably unavoidable, it does not help rebuild trust.

More positively, in both 2003 and 2007 many people told us we should feel flattered. A company whose deadly wares are peddled by prime ministers and royals felt worried enough by CAAT to mount spying operations. Maybe they saw that increasingly people do not want to give support to repressive regimes by selling them military equipment.

If BAE was worried then, perhaps it is even more so today as the Middle East descends into ever greater chaos and western military intervention is questioned. Hopefully, the day will soon dawn when David Cameron and Prince Charles' recent wooing of the autocratic Saudi Arabian royals to peddle arms will be acknowledged as unethical and misguided.

Then the skilled workers currently making military

equipment might use their ingenuity to address the need for clean renewable energy.

Ann Feltham
Parliamentary Co-ordinator
Campaign Against Arms Trade

# HELEN'S STORY

had a two year relationship with an undercover policeman who I knew as John Barker, his real name was John Dines.

In 1987 I got involved with an independent environmental and broadly anti-capitalist group. I met John there and over the next three years he became a close friend then we ended up in a relationship.

He told me about his dad's death and later asked to borrow money to go to his mum's funeral, told me he felt alone as an only child and how he'd lost his van and all his possessions. A clever combination of both sob stories and excuses for why there was nobody around him and why he didn't have any kind of history that you could see.

In reality, his mum was still alive, so was his dad, and he had brothers and sisters. His stories, eeking my empathy and involvement in his life, were a deliberate process of emotional manipulation. He was seeking to draw me closer to him, so that he could spy on me and my friends and seek to undermine the political movements we were involved in.

But I didn't know that at the time, I felt like I'd met my soul mate, and after a while we rented a flat and lived together. We talked about starting a family, he said he wanted lots of kids as he was an only child – and all the kind of things you might talk about in any normal relationship.

In the last six months of our relationship his behaviour became very erratic, he appeared to be going through some sort of breakdown. He would disappear saying he was taking himself off to sort his head out, then he would come back and declare how much he loved me – it was a very emotionally draining time.

Then he disappeared for good. I received two letters from him posted from South Africa, saying he was sorry, but he needed to sort his head out and if he did, he might come back.

I was extremely worried about his mental wellbeing and even worried that he might kill himself. And I was still deeply in love with him, so I spent ages trying to find out what had happened to him. But everything I investigated turned up more questions than answers and my concerns grew about who he really was and what he'd been up to. Then one day I had a sudden instinct to check death records, and found out he had been using the name of a child who'd died aged eight years old.

That left me with this great void. I'd been living with someone for two years and I now didn't even know what his name was. It threw all my other relationships into doubt – if you can live with someone for that length of time and think you know them so well, then you find out they don't even exist – what does it say for everybody else that you are talking to, that you are meeting with, how can you be sure that anything going on around you is real? How could I trust my own judgement any more? And try telling people what you think happened – the reaction is that you are paranoid, that couldn't happen here. Which makes you start to doubt your own sanity.

But this isn't just what happened to me, other women went through similar experiences. It causes serious psychological trauma. Some have suggested we've nothing much to complain about – men often lie about their age or background, we should just get over it. But there is a vast difference. This is an entirely false persona, a false name, false date of birth, false job, false personality, false politics, false marriage status (most of these cops were married). And to cap it all they are there to spy on you and your friends, and to try to undermine the movements for change that you support – it's a very real violation.

John disappeared in 1992 and I finally had confirmation that he was an undercover policeman in 2011. I had spent almost nineteen years trying to find out what had happened.

Around the same time, Mark Kennedy was exposed by campaigners as an undercover policeman. He'd had a seven-year relationship with a campaigner and other relationships too. The response of the police was to claim that he was a rogue police officer who had gone off the rails and done his own thing – it was an isolated incident. I was so angry at this I got together with other women who had long-term relationships with undercover policemen and we began legal action to expose the reality and try to stop it happening again. The eight of us involved in the case had relationships with five different officers over a period spanning about twenty-five years. And there are other people bringing cases too, some of them had children as a result of these deceptive relationships.

So despite police protestations, it's clear these relationships were an institutional tactic, not an individual one.

Since our case started and with the statements made by whistle blower Peter Francis (an ex-undercover cop in the Special Demonstration Squad), people have been shocked by the extent of police intrusion into people's lives, with revelations about spying on family campaigns for justice, including the family of murdered teenager Stephen Lawrence, and evidence of the police assisting with the blacklisting of trade unionists and other political campaigners.

It's important everyone is aware of the efforts by the state and powerful institutions to undermine movements for social progress, so we can all learn how to resist them. But it's also important not to let our own fear or suspicion of others undermine our efforts too. We should also take heart from the fact they do infiltrate our campaigns – it shows they know we can and do have an effect when we communicate with others about the change we want to see in the world. So keep on at it!

policespiesoutoflives.org.uk has more details about our case. We've also linked up with the Campaign Opposing Police Surveillance to work with other people and groups affected by undercover policing, campaignopposingpolice-surveillance.com.


Helen Steel
Police Spies Out of Our Lives

# GUY'S STORY

Simon Wellings was a slack bastard.

He rocked up to Globalise Resistance in 2001 and got involved in everything; local, international protests and innumerable planning meetings. In 2002 he was elected to the steering committee. He travelled to protests in New York, Seville, Geneva and all over Europe and the UK. He was always in the organising teams for actions, but rarely in the more analytical or theoretical conversations. He had a car, was never short of a few bob and was quickly deemed indispensable.

He forged good friendships with a number of us, sharing personal information, finding out frustrations, desires and things I shudder at the thought of being recorded in a file somewhere on Scotland Yard's server. He used to complain about not being able to get laid, that openness encouraging reciprocal sharing of similar info. He always came across as earnest and more than a little under-confident. He spent time with us outside the meetings and political actions, coming to a mate's place in Devon for a party over a weekend.

In January 2005 an activist emailed me an mp3 of a voicemail message. Listening to the message was unnerving. 'Yeah, he's done a lot of stuff for Globalise Resistance but flirts with the anarchist side of things' ... 'She's [name deleted]'s girlfriend, they're very overtly lesbian, they've been together for a long time.' It didn't take an expert to tell it was someone in the know being quizzed over images of protesters, giving information about relationships and connections between different activists, in GR and further afield. The background noises suggested they were in a police station. There were activists from across the spectrum mentioned and described. Sexuality and intimate relationships were especially noted.

I couldn't place the voice, but it sounded familiar. A couple of months later, stuffing envelopes in the office, listening to music on the computer, I took a phone call, muted the music and set up a planning meeting with Wellings.

Turning up the volume after the call, the music had shuffled onto the recording and the penny dropped.

The first words in the planning meeting we'd arranged were, 'Simon, you've been rumbled, fuck off'. He protested his innocence, he cried, he was almost convincing. Others cried, one or two decided he was innocent. We left it there – without a confession and with a small element of doubt, going public wasn't an option, and we didn't want to increase levels of paranoia amongst activists.

We eventually went public in 2011, Mark Kennedy/ Stone was in the news, undercover cops were being exposed. On the advice of the Ratcliffe protesters' solicitor it was time to go public with the phone message recording. Newsnight journalists were interested and published a picture of Wellings prominently on their website. The Met Police phoned and requested that Newsnight removed the picture. That request was enough to convince Newsnight's lawyers that Wellings was indeed a cop.

A slack bastard cop who made accidental phone calls at the most delicious of times.

Guy Taylor
Globalise Resistance

# DAVE'S STORY

B eing a member of a trade union is a perfectly legal activity enshrined in UN and EU human rights conventions. Yet it is hardly big news that major companies do not like union activists. Trade unionists have often complained about being victimised for standing up for their fellow workers. Sometimes reps get overlooked for promotion, occasionally they get sacked and in very exceptional cases activists find it impossible to get work with any firms in their chosen industry. For decades there have been rumours of blacklisting in the UK building industry but we were always accused of being paranoid conspiracy theorists.

But in 2009, the Information Commissioner's Office (ICO) raided the premises of an organisation called the Consulting Association and found the documentary evidence. Secret files held on 3,213 workers contained names, addresses, national insurance numbers, phone numbers, car registrations, photographs but also union membership and union credentials. The blacklist files contain press cuttings plus entries recording times when workers complained about unpaid wages or raised concerns about site safety. Other files record a union petition against homelessness, that someone was a Buddhist and even that an individual wore

Anti Nazi League badges! Some of the individual files are nearly fifty pages long.

The chief executive of The Consulting Association was Ian Kerr, who had previously worked for the notorious Economic League before it was closed down in the 1990s. But his paymasters were household names such as Balfour Beatty, Carillion, Kier, Costain, Laing O'Rourke and other major building contractors, who used the illegal database to check the names of prospective workers. If a name matched, the worker was refused work or sacked. Every time a firm checked a name they were charged around £2. In the last year of the Consulting Association, during the building of the Olympics Park, Sir Robert McAlpine and Skanska were both invoiced over £28,000 each: industrial scale blacklisting. The secret corporate spying organisation even had its own constitution that stipulated attendance at the quarterly meetings had to be at Director level.

For union activists this systematic blacklisting resulted in repeated dismissals and long periods of unemployment. Skilled workers lost their homes and had their children on free school meals, families divorced – all because they supported the union.

Most of the information on the blacklist files are attributed to senior managers but some entries came from corporate spies infiltrating union meetings. But it was not just multinationals that spied on us.

Ex-Special Demonstration Squad (SDS) undercover police officer Peter Francis (who spied on the Lawrence family) has given an interview to the *Guardian* confirming that he was instructed to spy on Frank Smith, a union and anti-racism activist. Frank Smith's blacklist file has an entry that reads 'under constant watch (officially) and considered to be politically dangerous', it also has information about his American girlfriend, who was also under surveillance by Francis. How would any manager on a building site know this personal sensitive information? Where would the information originate from, if not from the police? And this is not an isolated case. Campaigners have discovered there are a number of other blacklist files involving anti-racist and environmental campaigners that never worked on a building site in their life.

And Peter Francis is not the only example of police collusion. In the 1990s another undercover officer Mark Jenner posed as a building worker in east London, attending picket lines and even chairing construction safety campaign meetings. Unsurprisingly, extensive reports about activists who participated in these campaigns appear in their blacklist files. One of the people that Mark Jenner spied on was Steve Hedley, currently the Assistant General Secretary of the RMT union.

In 2008, an officer from the National Extremism Tactical Coordination Unit (NETCU) gave a PowerPoint presentation at a secret Consulting Association meeting. According to an interview Ian Kerr gave to *The Times*, the blacklisting body and secret police unit agreed a 'two-way exchange' of information. Notes of that meeting are held by the Information Commissioner's Office which has refused an FOI request to make them public.

The Blacklist Support Group submitted a complaint about police collusion to the IPCC. This has now been handed over to Operation Herne, the investigation into undercover policing. The IPCC have written back admitting that Special Branch officers across the UK routinely provided information about prospective employees.

Blacklisting is no longer an industrial relations issue; it is a conspiracy between multi-national construction firms, the police and the security services. The parallels with phone hacking are obvious. There is however a significant difference with phone hacking, where the police involvement was supposedly due to individual corruption. The police collusion in blacklisting is not one or two rogue officers but standard operating procedure by the state to target campaigners under the guise of 'domestic extremism' and routinely share information with big business.

If your politics are vaguely left of centre, it hardly comes as a big surprise that the state sides with big business against the trade unions. But in a democratic society, workers should be free to join a trade union and participate in peaceful protest without the fear that their every move will be recorded and that they will be denied the opportunity to provide for their families.

In any civilised society, the senior managers who deliberately orchestrated this conspiracy would be behind bars. But we live in a time when the pursuit of profit is valued above all else and the lives of real people, our children and partners, mean nothing to multinational corporations. I do not have a scintilla of respect for the directors who blacklisted two generations of union members. As for the cheerleaders and apologists in the legal and public relations professions, I wouldn't piss on them if they were on fire. But make no mistake. For those of us whose working lives have been ruined by these wretches, this is personal.

And we intend to hound these human rights abusers until we get justice.

Dave Smith
Blacklisted engineer
Blacklist Support Group

# THE
# RED SHED

# A NOTE FROM PETER HIRST

first met Mark when we were both students at Bretton
Hall Higher Education College, a place situated almost
exactly equidistant from Wakefield and Barnsley. The
college is long closed, but the buildings are still there and
the grounds are now famous as the Yorkshire Sculpture
Park. The college accommodation seems likely to become a
boutique hotel; a stately home built on the exploitation of
local coal and local people briefly available to all as a centre
of educational innovation under Alec Clegg,* now fated to
become an exclusive hotel for the monied.

Bretton, a manicured Capability Brown inspired velvet
rut. Students came from all over the country to study
there. I lived at home in Wakefield, with my girlfriend
from school. Mark came from London. *Fame* was on the
TV, the New Romantics were high in the charts. Bretton
Hall looked nice and clean and safe – it was like going on
holiday every week to a place where people had a chance
to make sense of themselves and their lives in comfort.
Mostly they were nice, clean middle-class people away from
home dyeing their hair, getting drunk for the first time and

---

* Sir Alexander Bradshaw Clegg, the Chief Education Officer for
West Riding of Yorkshire and a pioneer of radical educational
reforms.

losing their virginity – an opportunity everyone should have without the burden of debt.

I met some brilliant people there and saw that life was not bleak for everyone, everywhere. Some people had parents who were limited companies, some got cars for their eighteenth birthday, some people didn't get The Smiths.

While we were there, the callous, cruel and greedy policies of the eighties' free-marketeers were being introduced in Britain despite the calamities they had caused elsewhere in the world. Low taxes for the rich, greater trade freedom and privatisation of commonly-owned assets – an agenda that benefits only the super-rich and ruins the lives of everyone else and the planet itself. But those Tropicana drinks were free and Bretton College often looked like a place where the mantra was 'Fame costs, and this is where you start paying – in sweat'. The lie that hard work would be rewarded and everyone had an equal chance to self-expression, a career and leg-warmers – if only they would work hard! Two miles away Woolley Colliery was full of hardworking people whose reward would be to be vilified for fighting to protect their communities in a grim struggle for a decent life.

Bretton was a cocoon – all enthusiasm and art, very little politics, populated by comfortable, well-manicured, polite people, reminiscent of the Eloi in *The Time Machine*. And while Mark always rocked the leotard and alice band, he wasn't content to merely feed, play and mate.

Wakefield was a Tetley Bitter drinking town and the pubs were packed from Thursday through to Sunday with beered up locals pretending they were in a Duran Duran video. The Labour Club was not like this. At all. Ever.

It was a truth, universally accepted, that a young person in the eighties should be in search of a party to belong to. I joined the Labour Party and attended several meetings but somehow the detailed discussion of how best to resite bus stops on Park Lodge Lane seemed something of a distraction when the evils of Thatcherism were there to be fought. I was honestly amazed that anyone could even consider voting Conservative at any time, my reaction to election losses for Labour was not based on any real understanding of polling or policy – I was simply shocked. My parents were not particularly political, my dad was a Labour supporter of the old school 'fair day's work for a fair day's pay', he was a fan of Harold Wilson. He didn't do anything political except vote and read the *Daily Mirror*.

Mark and I were kindred spirits, eager and restless – doers, not talkers – and so we set off on a political Odyssey with the Labour Club as our Argos. We fought for the miners, for student grants, for CND and against union busters. For Cuba, against nursery closures, for anti-apartheid. We met wonderful, wonderful people.

Those of us who believe that we have a responsibility to leave the world and the people in it in better condition than we found it, need positive stories and places where those stories will get heard. A repository of hope, where the belief is that, in the end, our endeavours will result in a world that is a fairer and better place. Far too much of the storytelling has been in the hands of the media, owned and controlled by those with a big share in the status quo.

The Red Shed is full of stories that are not known or celebrated, but this is the place where Mark and I chose to go and still choose to go. London is many towns all accreted together. Bretton an educational pastoral idyll. Wakefield town centre full of places where many drank to forget – but the Red Shed is, at its best, a place to go to remember and to use that memory to draw strength for other challenges. To remember that nothing worth having ever came easy, to remember the heroism of struggle and the joy of solidarity even in defeat.

Maybe the Labour Club was the start of Mark's political and performance journey, but Mark's search for truth and justice began a long time before he came to Bretton Hall, Wakefield or the Red Shed – not that it matters. It doesn't matter because his commitment, loyalty and love for the club has sustained the club and energised the fiftieth anniversary celebrations and those of us who have joined him on his search for the schoolkid singers and the school.

Peter R Hirst

# A NOTE FROM RICHARD COUNCIL, SECRETARY OF THE RED SHED

Who would have believed that a red shed could be on Broadway! Well not quite, but you don't know.

Fifty years a socialist club, never a derogatory description of us and genuinely true for the thirty-four years I have been a member.

We have seen good times and bad, many battles both local and national, a financial fight for our survival and just as importantly, we are still here to tell the tale.

The club is a living and breathing entity which spans politics across the left – has seen the occasional Tory councillor and MP cross our doors (and buy a round for those in the bar!). We are the home of new music, of environmental politics, of good real ale and CAMRA, the local TUC, trade unions and even the Labour Party and so much else.

We are proud of all of this.

We are a simple wooden building purchased and supported by Labour Party members since September 1966.

Many of the great and the good have visited us. I remember being on car parking duty for Dennis Skinner and door warden for Ken Livingstone. The club has enemies as well as friends and we have always known this, but we persevere. From 1966 to 2016, it is interesting the things that have stayed the same in politics and also those that have changed. The club has seen them all and lived through the social upheaval of the last half century.

But above all we are a social club. A place of safety, of respect and heated but not violent debate. A place where people can be very different but walk away as friends and still fighting for the things they believe in.

There have been many characters over the years, some of them mentioned in Mark Thomas' production today. Colin Marsh, legendary President of the club and known as Chairman Mao. Eddie Lee, who slept in the club and bankrolled us for a time as Secretary. Byron Cassar, the meanest Greek Club Steward west of Athens whose glare could chill a young socialist at twenty paces, and indeed our own current president, George Denton, who seems to have more ailments than a medical dictionary but still manages to be ever present, ever faithful.

There has been a history of struggle throughout, such as the construction workers' dispute in the seventies and the miners' strike in the eighties. The glory of the night in 1997 when Labour won a landslide election and the disillusion that followed with a socialist government that never was.

There have been environmental campaigns like Pugney's Action Group, unknown outside Wakefield but important nonetheless to those who live here. Greater conflict over South African apartheid and gay rights. The combat operation to save Sandal nursery which spawned a generation of new activists and a seemingly endless drip, drip, drip of cuts to public services and those who provide them. For all these things the club was there!

So now in our fiftieth year where are we? Well, we stand alone as a city centre club – all the other social clubs worthy of the name, have gone.

But the values that drove our forefathers (and mothers) live on. From the campaign to confront fracking, to the fight for trade unionising fast food and retail outlets – we had a live link with the USA for the Bakers' Union in April – and of course the inimitable influence of our Red Shed Players, pantomime king, Peter Hirst with Wakefield Trades Council and Mark Thomas trailblazing for us in this production.

Being a club promoting the philosophy of the left has never been easy and it probably will never be. There are so many characters who have brightened our lives and so many who are no longer with us. But that philosophy lives on.

In our fiftieth year we have made it a policy to promote the inclusion of young people, are looking at our accessibility to the disabled, continue to promote socialist education and preserve our history and our members, more than 500 of them, continue to support the fun, the fights and the freedoms we project. Not to mention excellent, well priced ale.

So what for the future? Times are now more uncertain than ever but we have a stable and committed committee who will continue to power the club onwards. We will celebrate our anniversary in September with a mixture of politics, comedy, music and just generally having a good time and, at the time of writing, we are looking forward to the hard work that this will cause.

The club committee over the years has played a varying role in the management of the club. The current set up is more hands on than at any previous juncture, but all of us love it and believe in the cause. I believe all that served before us did so as well and thank them for their commitment. Members of the current committee deserve mentioning. There is our darling of the Saturday lunchtime crowd and Treasurer, Jan Samuel. 'Big' Steve Wiltshire, our Saturday night anchor-man. Vice President and technology whizz kid, Matty Hallas. Our resident electrician and handyman, Sam Eldridge. Glass washer par excellence, Vic Wilkins and our Tuesday dynamic 'husband and wife' duo, Phil and Carol Pinnell. 'H' Riley manages the transport with his yellow van, Paul Holmes and Ian Bain are committee regulars and keep us on our toes. We even have our own Wakefield Councillor on hand, Kevin Swift to fight our cause and steer us in the right direction. Everyone has a role and is valued for their involvement in the day-to-day management of the club.

Our stewardship of the club must be to perpetuate a unique institution and project the beliefs and energies of those that went before us into a new history.

Here is to the next fifty years, in our Red Shed.

Richard Council
Secretary
Wakefield Labour Club
2016

# THE RED SHED

*Onstage a set of red doors, four seats and a table either side of the stage towards the front.*

*Before audience comes in MT has talked to crowd in the bar as they wait and got six volunteers to come and sit on stage.\* Each one gets a red card, they give it to the usher when they go in. Usher shows them to seats near front so they can easily come onstage. They also will have been taken onstage before the show, shown the masks, where the chairs will go, and where to line up and put banner.*

*Also some party poppers are given out.*

---

\* For me, the show starts when I walk out into the bar thirty minutes before the curtain goes up. I will chat to the audience and ask six of them to join me onstage to help make the show. I want very specific types of people. During the Edinburgh Festival, for example, I would always ask eager volunteers if they were performing in other shows at the Fringe, if they were then they were politely disinvited. The volunteers must be comfortable onstage but must not look too keen and they must reflect the audience. Once chosen, I will take the six people through to the stage and show them roughly what will happen. I will check they are comfortable with the tasks I am going to give them, as I don't want anyone there against their wishes. I want the people onstage with me to feel that they have helped create the show.

# PROLOGUE

Welcome, in tonight's performance I am being assisted by six members of the audience who I spoke to in the queue. Would they come on stage please?

*ADDRESSES AUDIENCE:* I need your help too with some songs, whistles, noises and shouts. At one point I'm going to divide the audience in two.

This side of the audience *INDICATES* you are the 'rhubarb orchestra' your job is to sound like the bar in the Red Shed and you go 'rhubarb rhubarb rhubarb'.

*LEADS HALF OF AUDIENCE IN PRACTICE* – you can ad lib over the top a few 'cheers' 'ey up' 'oi oi', improvise but don't go jazz.

This half *INDICATES OTHER SIDE* you are the 'here we go' choir.

*LEADS OTHER HALF OF AUDIENCE IN PRACTICE*

OK.

*ADDRESSES SEATED VOLUNTEERS:* Right, if you are all comfortable, let's start.

In 1989 I did an interview with a journalist from the *NME*\*

---

\* Andrew Collins.

it was on comics to look out for in the future, I was listed alongside Bill Hicks, Eddie Izzard and Jo Brand, I know I have somewhat let the side down.

I know what the journalist wants, stories, who you are? Where are you from? What have you done? The first this, the first that. And I have those stories, I am made up of stories.

The first time I used who I am and where I am from was aged four. I went up to a police officer directing traffic at the junction of Northcote Road and Clapham Junction and said,

'Excuse me Mr Policeman my name is Mark Clifford Thomas I live at 12 Kyrle Road and my telephone number is 228 1528 and I have lost my mum.'

My dad when he came to collect me says the cop is standing in the middle of the road, one arm around me, directing traffic with the other.

My mum says I was helping direct the traffic.

First part in school nativity play, Innkeeper.

My first band Queen, 1976, second band Dr Feelgood, third Siouxsie and the Banshees. Quite a learning curve.

First sex with a woman sixteen behind a cinema, second time in a multi-storey car park, third graveyard. Fairly traditional upbringing. Quite conservative.

First demo was CND demo in Morden.

First picket line *Stockport Messenger* dispute,* Warrington. In the flame-lit road of an industrial estate where the police had baton charged the pickets I saw a Scot with a massive head wound and blood over his shirtless torso shouting at the police,

'I wasnae a communist when I come here but I am now!'

First public performance in the Red Shed, Wakefield.

First stand-up gig 1985† White Lion, Putney – act on before me, Andy Johnson. His stage name was Cyril the Tortoise, he would impersonate tortoises for twenty minutes. A different age. And if he was booked to do thirty minutes, he would put a couple of tea strainers over his eyes and do a bee as a filler for ten.

I have got the stories.

But the journalist asks, 'Where did you get your politics from?'

'Miners' strike, I was at college in Yorkshire and got involved.'

And then the words began to fly out ...

---

* After Eddie Shah, owner of *Today* newspaper, challenged the closed shop agreement and used non-union labour. It was the first time Thatcher's anti-union legislation was used and it was a brutal episode. Years later, I did an interview with the *Warrington Guardian* and the journalist asked whether I'd been to Warrington before. I said I had, during the *Stockport Messenger* dispute, and recounted the police brutality and the fear I felt as a police truncheon battered the window of the van I was in. Without missing a beat, the journo came back with, 'So, did you enjoy your visit?'
† 19 November.

... Miners I got to know arrested on trumped up charges, found guilty in kangaroo courts and convictions reversed on appeal but still lost their pensions ...

... police riots at Orgreave.* BBC found guilty of falsely reporting, Labour Party leadership, Neil Kinnock cutting the miners off at the knees ...

... 140,000 miners on strike for a year, with no wages, union assets frozen in the courts, no dole, so include their families and half-a-million people were being fed in soup kitchens ...

... and the cops – the London Met – waving their pay packets at people fed in soup kitchens ...

The facts come spluttering out, half remembered, half formed, struggling to get to the surface in the white heat of molten memory.

---

* The most brutal and violent episode in the miners' strike. On 18 June 1986, police charged picketing miners, beating them with batons. The BBC edited the sequence of its footage resulting in a more favourable version of events for the police. Ninety-five people were charged with rioting, but the trial collapsed when it became clear that the evidence had been fabricated by South Yorkshire police force, who would go on to do the same at Hillsborough. Had justice been done and the police held to account for their lies, the Hillsborough cover up could not have happened.

Amber Rudd, the Home Secretary, indicated that she would be open to some kind of inquiry to establish the truth but then defied expectations and blocked the inquiry. As I was performing in her constituency a few days later, I invited her to the show (free tickets – you know what they are like, they'll not come if they have to pay). She didn't turn up but the Orgreave Truth and Justice Campaign and Kent NUM did. I am delighted the Orgreave Truth and Justice Campaign has turned up to run stalls at the show on a few occasions. SALUT!

And then I recall an incident, not yet a story as this is the first time it is remembered. At the end of the year-long strike the miners marched back to work, through pit villages to the colliery.

I was invited to a march back, I do not remember the name of the village or the pit or the woman who asked me along. But I do remember we march uphill, somewhere in the distance is the National Union of Mineworkers' banner, a band playing, half carnival half funeral, the village line the streets, clapping,

'Well done, well done.'

And sometimes they shout individuals' names,

'Well done Ian, head up.'

We walk past a school, a Victorian looking school, with big eaves, steep roofs and the playground has iron bars and concrete humps that the iron is sunk into and the kids, aged somewhere between five and ten, are in the playground, standing on the concrete and holding onto the iron railings and they're singing through the bars to the miners as they march back to work:

*SINGS CHORUS FROM 'SOLIDARITY FOREVER'*

They are singing to their fathers, their uncles, their brothers, their community.

*SINGS FIRST TWO LINES FROM 'SOLIDARITY FOREVER'*

I don't know where they learnt this song, maybe they are copying older kids or maybe they have sung this song on rallies and events. But they seem to be singing into the face of defeat, singing into the future, to a better time, they sing a sliver of hope.

And once you have witnessed that, a door opens that can never be shut.

And I have told that story so many times since, I have forgotten how much of it is true. You get a story, give it a polish and bits of the truth fall off, one night you improvise out a line and it gets a good reaction, the next night it stays in the story and is suddenly 'true'.

I love telling stories and don't mind little fibs of expediency. I've told you two already. In the list of stories ...

I was never an innkeeper. Joseph. Husband of the mother of Jesus.

Also I have never had sex in a graveyard. Never. Multi-storey car park, every level. Graveyard never.

So in this show I am going to try and find the village and the school and I am going to try and find the children to see how much of this story is true.

Because, and I say this quietly and with great reluctance, Michael Gove is right. If you say I said that outside this theatre and I will sue every one of you.

Gove is right,

'People in this country have had enough of experts.'*

We don't like facts getting in the way of our stories. If truth makes an appearance it is as a walk-on part, a cameo, then it is off.

But the stories we tell, the stories politicians tell, the stories communities tell don't just declare who we are and where we are from but what our intentions are, what we are going to do. They shape our future, so my story had better be true.

By the way this is a show about the miners' strike but there is no brass band music or kids discovering a penchant for ballet.

---

* Michael Gove – Tory outrider for alternative facts.

# PART 1

It is celebration time in the Red Shed.

*ORCHESTRATES HALF THE AUDIENCE TO
MAKE RHUBARB\* NOISE AND THE OTHER HALF
TO SING 'HERE WE GO', AT THE CRESCENDO
PARTY POPPERS ARE FIRED FROM THE CROWD*

*NB – LET THE RHUBARB AND THE 'CHEERS'
DEVELOP*

It is the 8th April 2013, Margaret Thatcher has just died.

*PICKS UP AN EDIROL 09 FROM TABLE*

Now this is an Edirol 09 – it is a digital recorder – I bought
mine in 2004 – it has history. It has travelled the entire
length of the Israeli wall in the West Bank and recorded
everyone I spoke to. It has been teargassed in Turkey and
chased gang masters in El Salvador. It has also been left on

---

\* Wakefield is well known for its rhubarb, forms part of the
Rhubarb Triangle and has a rhubarb festival in February each year. I
have been told that in the rhubarb sheds of Wakefield 'You can hear
it growing'.

a bus and left on a plane, and once used in anger against me when my children secretly recorded me singing, Elvis Presley's 'In the Ghetto'.

Now finally it comes home and heads to Yorkshire to the Red Shed to record my friends.

*PLAYS EDIROL:*

**PETE: If something happens, whether a strike or Margaret Thatcher dies, or something happens like that, you would be able to go to down to the Shed and there will be like-minded people ready to do something about it.**

This is Peter, one of my best chums, I met him when I was 18. This is Andy Gough, ex-president of the Red Shed.

*PLAYS EDIROL:*

**ANDY: When Thatcher died you'd be surprised it were just like an old meeting, you automatically came here. I went for pint up town and I thought, I know where I need to be.**

The Red Shed is in Wakefield, a town that lies between Leeds and Barnsley in Yorkshire.

First time I go into a pub in Barnsley there is a picture of Mohammed Ali torn from a newspaper on the wall and underneath a hand written note, 'HE GETS PAID A MILLION QUID TO FIGHT, YOU GET BARRED.'

I arrive in Wakefield as an eighteen-year-old student from south London. To get the Red Shed in 1981, turn left out of

Wakefield Westgate station and walk the High Road, there are nineteen pubs in the space of one mile – this is a party town and people have money to burn – go past Casanova's nightclub, 'No Jeans, No Trainers and mobile shower unit for Miss Wet T-Shirts competitions'. When there were complaints the club said,

'Aye aye aye, there's not discrimination here, we've got Mr Wet Y-Fronts.'

Shrink-wrapped offal in a wet cloth jiggling to the sounds of 'Agadoo'.*

Go past the run of clubs and you reach the bus station, turn right and head through the market and there in Vicarage Street is the Red Shed. It is what it says it is – it is red, it is a shed. It is a wooden, single storey, forty-seven-foot long socialist shed fifty years old this September. Opposite the Tory club. Two storeys high, brick and shut. The Red Shed is an improbable survivor in the gale of globalization, bathed literally as we speak in the neon glow of a Debenhams' sign on the side of the shopping centre.

These are the actual chairs from the club, they kindly lent them, so those stains you are sitting on, that's genuine socialist arse sweat.

---

* The promotional video for Agadoo's 'Superman' was shot in Casanova's. I didn't know that at the time. The other notable thing about Casanova's was that it had a telephone on each table – this was before mobile phones – and each telephone had a large piece of plastic with a number on it so you could see someone you fancied on the other side of the club and call them. Which invariably led to a lot of calls starting, 'NO, not you, the one with the good 'air!'

The doors, they would not lend me. We had to make our own.

## WALKS BEHIND DOORS AND ENTERS THROUGH THEM

On the inside of the door is a hand written note, 'Put Wood in t'hole' – means shut the door.

In front of you is a noticeboard. Here *INDICATES* the bar. The club is forty-seven foot long and eighteen feet wide, the bar is eighteen feet by fourteen feet. Here *INDICATES* is the small committee room twelve feet and then the big committee room twenty-one feet.

The rooms are divided by folding wooden doors, so the club can be opened in any configuration.

On the walls ceramic plates commemorating strikes and struggles, over the bar a large glass case displaying trade union badges from across the world and a brass plaque commemorating Byron Cassar. Byron was a club steward, a Greek Stalinist, who had fought Nazis, the Generals in Greece and helped unionise the merchant seamen. He washed up in Wakefield and had a combination Greek/ Yorkshire accent, you would often hear,

'We must continue the struggle, uh eye.'

He held no elected official in respect and if a Labour councillor came to a meeting and tried to pay for a round of drinks with a £20 note,

'What do you think this is, Barclays fucking Bank!'

My first time in the Shed someone said be careful of Byron, he doesn't like students, especially from the south.

'Pint please.'

'You are a student?'

'Yes.'

'You are here for the trade union meeting?'

'Yes.'

'You are the future!'

I have never been so terrified of the future.*

I am invited to attend a Red Shed committee meeting at the end of last year.

*SITS AT TABLE WITH THREE AUDIENCE MEMBERS STAGE LEFT, ADDRESSES AUDIENCE MEMBER AT END OF ROW:* You're George, if you could lift your mask up, face the audience, thank you.

George is the club President he says,

'Right then best of order. Minutes of last meeting approved? Carried. Main item club's fiftieth anniversary year and celebration plans.'

*ADDRESSES NEXT AUDIENCE MEMBER:* You're Peter.

---

* I once took Robert Newman to the Red Shed, after a gig in Wakefield. As I walked in the barman said, 'Alright Mark d'you want one of your waters? Robert what can I get you?'
 Robert replied, 'A gin and tonic with ice and lemon.'
 And the barman said, 'FRUIT?!'

*INDICATES TO AUDIENCE VOLUNTEER WITH MASK* As you can see he has been in the wars in this picture. I wish I could say he did it in some noble fashion like fighting fascists but he dropped a bottle of beer and it bounced back and broke his nose.

Peter says,

'I think we need to be energising all the new members who have joined as a result of Jeremy Corbyn becoming leader. We need to have a series of talks, political events and lectures that will get people into the Shed and get them active in local as well as national politics.'

*ADDRESSES FINAL AUDIENCE VOLUNTEER:* You're David.

I say,

'... and we should be working with the Bakers' Union,* there's no mines, steel and textiles but there are plenty of people working in fast food and they have no union and zero hour contracts and poor pay, the Bakers' Union is trying to unionise them and we should be supportive of that ... And I also would like to do a show about the Shed.'

Everyone looks at me.

*ADDRESS AUDIENCE VOLUNTEERS IN MASKS IF NEEDED:* Look at me.

---

* Wakefield has 119.5 fast food outlets per 100,000 inhabitants: one of the highest in the UK. In alliance with campaigns globally, the Bakers' Union is campaigning for better working conditions and £10 an hour for all fast food workers.

Takes a breath.

*ADDRESS AUDIENCE VOLUNTEERS IN MASKS IF NEEDED:* Take a breath.

And then looks back.

*ADDRESS AUDIENCE VOLUNTEERS IN MASKS IF NEEDED:* Look back.

David is the ex-Labour MP for the area and like most Labour MPs he improves with resignation.*

'I think you're right about fast food workers but as you get older you want to reflect on what you have done, to assess what you have achieved. I think we should bring out a book to celebrate all the great men and women who have made this club. Now if you're doing a show you have to include them.'

David says,

'Miners' strike. Very important. We supported 150 families from this club.'

Someone else says,

'And ban the bomb.'

David says,

'And ban the bomb, very popular. And don't forget the anti-apartheid movement, we had buses leave this shed for

---

* David played Rugby League until concussion after a match persuaded him to retire. He's the author of *Rugby's Class Wars* and a former Chair of the National Coal Mining Museum.

every demo. Don't forget the local campaigns. The Pugney's environmental campaign started here. The narrow boat collective started here. Folk club. Bygone bikes. The gays started here.'

I think people were gay before the club.

'No, no they had their first public meeting here.'

So gays in Wakefield didn't come out of the closet but out of the Shed?

'Exactly.'

I have been coming back here since I was nineteen, I have performed here, organised demos, campaigned against PFI hospitals, attended meetings.

I love this place. This tiny hut is bigger than the sum of its parts. It is like a Tardis but one that only goes backwards in time. And for the first time since coming here for thirty-four years I worry this place is becoming quaint.

A wooden time capsule, a nostalgia cocoon where you can nurse pints and relive noble defeats.

For the first time I feel there is too much history here.

Peter is more considered.

*PLAYS EDIROL:*

PETER: The modern world is all about making you forget, isn't it? It is all about you're in this immediate moment and then it's gone.

Anyone who has ever taken a photo of their meal and put it on Twitter that is you.

*PLAYS EDIROL:*

**PETER: Whereas the Shed, all the badges and the plates from the miners' strike and the sea strike, and everything else like that ...**

Exactly the things I am currently questioning.

*PLAYS EDIROL:*

**PETER: ... it places you in a historical struggle. It has got that kind of sense that you are part of a history. And this history is genuine and it is about people and about how people have worked hard to make their lives better and sometimes that is through politics and sometimes that is through social and artistic pursuits.**

Peter and I have history.

I went to college near Wakefield, Bretton Hall, arts and education. I was a drama student. Now I know when you say the words, 'I am a drama student,' what you are actually saying is, 'we are not going to be talking about you for about two hours.'

I was a drama student, I have a degree, I have a BA Hons in ME!

Peter and I were introduced by my friend Anita,*

---

* I owe her a cup of tea.

'I think you and Peter should meet you're so similar. Very simpatico. Both gobby, bit out there, don't mind giving it out. Even if you don't like each other it should be entertaining.'

Two days later in a canteen,

'Peter, Mark. Mark, Peter. Stands back to enjoy.'

'Nah then lad is tha' from that there London?'

'I am.'

'One of them middle-class bastards come up here to slum it in t'north.'

'You're from Wakefield?'

'Aye, Wakey born Wakey bred, strong in arm thick in head.'

'And sexist in T-shirt.'

He is wearing a mermaids of bondage T-shirt, with a pen and ink drawing of a mermaid with pierced nipples, bound hands and an improbable strap on tail.

That is a sexist T-shirt.

'Now then I think tha' what tha's confusing is sexuality and sexism. This T-shirt depicts a cartoon retro vision of sado-masochism. Now when tha' confuses and conflates sexuality with the oppression of women then if anything it's tha' who's being the sexist.'

I liked him and it set the template for our relatiu ıship. He had a love of language that came from being working class and educated. I once had a mohican which I dyed blond – drama student.

'What the bloody hell is that tonsorial aberration?'*

Peter and I formed a left wing student radical theatre group, we would write in an afternoon and perform in the evening, refusing to rehearse, believing that to be bourgeois affectation. Our slogan was, 'Preparation NO, Improvisation, maybe ...'

As we were a radical theatre group, in every other show I would play the role of US intervention in Central America. I'd wear a cowboy hat, walk on,

'I am US intervention!'

Peter would twirl moustaches,

'I am evil capitalist.'

And his brother Joe who was scrawnier,

'I am noble but oppressed proletariat.'

That was the lexicon we were working with.

Our shows were always to raise money for causes and campaigns and we would perform anywhere we could –

---

* The principal of the college, a man called Dr Taylor, was also an architect. One summer holiday, he visited apartheid South Africa on a lecture tour. At the time, I was the editor of the student magazine along with my mate, Brian Hallett, and we got a cartoonist to do the front cover – a smiling Dr Taylor offering 'cardboard flexi-ghettos' to the hordes of Soweto. We handed out 500 free copies before we were summoned to the principal's office where a quaking Dr Taylor ranted at us and threatened to take us to court. Peter was our student union rep and was in the meeting, he calmly looked the principal in the eye and said, 'That'll look good in't *Guardian*. "Principal takes students to court".'
We never heard another word from Dr Taylor.

working men's clubs, social clubs, churches, miners' soup kitchens. But our home gig was the Red Shed. Surrounded by friends, comrades, trade unionists, commies, trots, feminists, veggies, greens, drunks and an assortment of folk who didn't fit in anywhere else. And nothing keeps you on your toes like a hairy-arsed miner standing up mid-monologue saying,

'I'm just going for a pint, don't wait for me.'*

At the end of the miners' strike I was in a student bar and a young miner I know called Ian comes in,

'Mark, we're going back to work and we had a meeting tonight. At the end of the meeting everyone were given an enamel badge to commemorate the strike and we had three strike breakers at our pit. They're not getting badges so we had a vote and it were decided that two should go to the students for their support in the strike, so on behalf of North Gawber NUM I would like to present this to you.'

And he hands me a red plastic box, inside a foam backing and an enamel badge, a gold pit head against a black circle and a red outer circle with the words 'North Gawber NUM Strike 84–85'.

Then he gives the other one to another student who has had nothing to do with the strike, or supporting the miners, in

---

* Only gag I remember is:
  Two men walk onstage.
  First person: Do you want to buy a ticket for the policeman's ball?
  Second: No thanks, I don't dance.
  First: It's not a dance, it's a raffle.

fact she says she is apolitical – 'apolitical' that is Tory for 'I don't want an argument'. Peter is incandescent.

'She got a badge! She did nowt. My badge. She. She's got my badge. A Tory. They give my fucking badge to a fucking Tory! No wonder they lost the strike.'

This has gone on for thirty-two years. And it has got so bad that on a couple of occasions I have offered my badge.

'I don't want your badge. I want my badge. The one she took from me!'*

---

* The man who gave me the North Gawber badge is Ian Nichols. He still lives in the area and the first thing he said when I spoke to him on the phone was, 'Has thou still got that badge I give thee?'

# PART 2

So I decide to help celebrate the Red Shed's fiftieth birthday, I will commit a number of tasks:

I will help Peter organise the speakers and events for the Shed.

I will attempt to find common cause with the Bakers' Union.

I will find the school and those children who sang through the bars of the school playground.

I am aware this is a somewhat saccharine image – urchins, singing, through bars, and I do not want to romanticise the working class. I'll have no truck with that nonsense that every human action can be judged to be good or bad entirely on the class of the person doing it. Frankly that is just a parlour game of the Left – 'prolier than thou'.

During the strike at Barnsley FC home games sections of the crowd would chant,

'I'd rather be a nigger than a scab.'

So who wants to be first in line to get misty-eyed over that particular piece of working-class nostalgia?

But if we are to defeat the rising tide of racism and the whiff of fascism then we are not going to do so by pointing the finger and saying, they believe in myths, they believe in fairy stories, they believe in a vision of the 1950s that never existed. If we are to challenge that myth then our narrative, my narrative has to be true.

I am also going to find that badge for Peter and get him to shut the fuck up after thirty-two years.

I start my quests on that most unreliable repository of memory Facebook. I find the woman who has the other badge. I take a photo of the badge I still have. I mail a message,

> Hi Mark here, remember this badge, you and I were presented with one each in the bar? I have mine. Do you still have yours?

She replies,

> No, haven't got it. Don't remember.

Nononononono.

I have failed at the first hurdle.

Things go slightly better with the Bakers' Union. I hook up with a union organiser, Gareth …

*LIFTS UP A CLIPBOARD WITH GARETH'S FACE ON THE BACK*

… and I ask him, how on earth do you unionise in the fast food industry, when it's not as if they want unions there?

He says, 'Come with me, I'll take you round Wakey.'

We head around Wakefield to every fast food outlet: Café Nero, Costa, Subway, Pizza Hut … By the way Greggs is unionised, they have national agreements and negotiations, paid holidays and fixed contracts … I have waited so long for a political excuse for those sausage rolls. Wahey! This isn't gluttony this is solidarity!

We go into KFC straight up to the manager,

'Excuse me, boss, we're doing a petition to get the government to pay £10 an hour minimum wage, can we ask your workers if they would sign it?'

The manager says, 'I'll bloody sign. £10 an hour! I'll take it round and make sure they sign.'

He comes back with the signatures of all the workers, who have included their contact details. And once they finish their shifts Gareth can contact them and that is where you start.

As for the children, I send out a clarion call to all true men and women of Yorkshire with memories of conscience, to stir their visions of the past and bring forth the facts. And to that end I go on BBC Radio Leeds Breakfast show.

'Right with me now in the studio is Mark Thomas. Now you're chasing children.'

NOT ON THE BBC.

NOT IN LEEDS.

I clarify the story about trying to find the children who sang in the schoolyard and how I want to speak to people about that event.

And the message goes out across the county of Yorkshire, down Denby Dale, along the Calder Valley, across the moor and back again. And BBC Radio Leeds beat their record for listener response ... no one calls in. They have never had it so low.

Articles appear in the print media of the *Barnsley Chronicle* and the *Wakefield Express* again, no one responds.

And so it is that I have to find the village the pit, the school, the children myself.

I cannot remember the village or the pit but the one thing I remember is this village was no more than a forty-minute bus journey from where I used to live in Wakey. So I got a large map of the area and drew a circle around it, which is the distance I estimate a forty-minute bus journey to be. Any pits in that area are a potential target – there were twenty-seven pits within a forty-minute bus journey from where I used to live. So I must go round and find these pits, not easy as they are no longer in existence. If there is a school nearby, see if the route for the march back to work goes past the school. If it does I walk the route and see if anything jogs my memory. Find the school, find the teachers, find the children, find if the story is true.

For a quest such as this I call upon my friends and comrades.

*MOVES TWO CHAIRS TO CENTRE*

*ADDRESSES AUDIENCE VOLUNTEER STAGE RIGHT:* Peter, would you sit here?

*ADDRESSES AUDIENCE VOLUNTEER STAGE LEFT:*
Will you bring Sandra's mask and sit here?

*GETS THIRD CHAIR PLACES IT BEHIND THEIRS*
*AND KNEELS ON IT*

I first met Sandra when I was nineteen and it seemed liked I had known her forever. She left school at fifteen, she became a dinner lady and before she had turned twenty-three she had visited Moscow to study Russian Literature, been accepted on the British Youth Council delegation to visit Cuba, been thrown off the British Youth Council delegation by a young Peter Mandelson – a badge of honour for any political persuasion – been reinstated on the British Youth Council by the Cuban Embassy and then greeted on arrival as a plucky schoolgirl hero fighting to reach the socialist motherland. She also has a car and often brings a picnic.

*ADDRESSES AUDIENCE VOLUNTEER PLAYING*
*PETER:* Before we go, I am sitting in the front, so if you have this mask and be me and I will be Peter.

*HANDS AUDIENCE VOLUNTEER A MARK*
*THOMAS MASK AND TAKES THE PETER MASK*

Sandra drives.

*ADDRESSES AUDIENCE VOLUNTEER PLAYING*
*SANDRA:* Could you drive?

The pitheads are long landscaped away, the industry and the community it spawned airbrushed with all the dignity of a motorway verge.

At Dearne Valley colliery all that is left is a stone, 'Dearne Valley colliery 1901'.\*

At Barnsley Main,† nothing, nothing but a set of colliery gates standing by themselves in wasteland. Were this three miles down the road in the Yorkshire Sculpture Park you'd charge £15 and say it's an Ai Weiwei.

At Goldthorpe‡ we can't find any evidence at all of where the pit was so Sandra pulls over. Unwinds the window.

*ADDRESSES AUDIENCE VOLUNTEER:* Use the button, use the button.

She leans out the window and asks for directions.

'Excuse me, love, do you know where the pit was?'

Half-a-dozen people reply.

Armed with directions we stop at lights, and in front of us is a school, Victorian looking, steep eaves, iron bars. I photograph it, as Sandra drives off.

*ADDRESSES AUDIENCE VOLUNTEER PLAYING MT:* Could you take a photo?

I have a map to get to Woolley Colliery§ drawn by local artist John Ledger. It is a piece of paper and a single black pen line and a list of landmarks that we will pass – Dalton, football pitch, posh house.

---

\* Shut 1989.
† Shut 1991.
‡ Shut 1994.
§ Shut 1987.

'"Posh House" ... how are we to find ... oh it's there! ... the one with a balcony.'

We arrive at Woolley* Colliery.

*ADDRESSES AUDIENCE VOLUNTEERS:* Would you take the seats back to table?

Now during the strike when the police began to assemble on picket lines, pickets and demonstrators would whistle and hum an old Laurel and Hardy tune.

*WHISTLES TUNE†*

*ADDRESSES AUDIENCE:* All together and if you can't whistle hum it, on three for practice.

*PRACTICE WHISTLE*

*ADDRESSES AUDIENCE:* Great. I'll cue you in in a minute. You keep it going, I'll tell the story over the top, you do the soundtrack, and tell you when to stop.

---

\* When we arrived at Woolley, Peter remembered that we had done a collection for the miners at the beginning of the strike and had turned up to present them with trays of beer and money. We were treated like heroes. Sometime later, we turned up with 'left over catering' from a student conference, which had been deliberately over-ordered so we could help the miners with the excess. Unfortunately, the catering had been done by the Whole Food Society and where once we had been greeted with cheers we were now greeted with the words, 'What th'fuck is mung beans?!'

† At this point, any ex-miners in the audience would join in and start whistling before I'd asked the audience to join in.

At Woolley Peter has a flashback, 'We were here, six of us, we came to support the picket and it were so early it was dark. The braziers were literally here. And as the sun came up the cops started to line up literally here. And from behind us we hear ...'

*MT CUE WHISTLING:* On three. Keep it going, I'll tell you when to stop.

Behind us hundreds of miners getting ready for the morning rush and shove.

*ADDRESSES AUDIENCE:* Keep it going.

Suddenly from the top of the hill a solitary police van with the one strike-breaking miner appears ... and the whistling stops ... There is a clatter of boots, then WHOOOAAAA and Peter and I are pushed through the police line, past one, two, three lines of cops. And we pop out on the other side of the police line, the place where everyone else wants to be, the only ones to have made it, surrounded by cops with truncheons. The van with the strike-breaker comes past and we shout,

'Scab! ... We're drama students. Not in the face, not in the face!'

Peter leads Sandra and I up a rough asphalt path running along allotments, sheds, chicken coops, tied dogs and beds of the white bulbs and green stalks of leeks emerging from the earth.

He says,

'D'you remember coming here on the march back? We walked along the High Road, came over the hill and through these woods, you remember?'

He stares at me,

'We were here.'

His eyes are wide with expectation. And I realise Peter is trying to drag me into his memory.

'We were on the march back here.'

He gazes with the look of a zealot awaiting my 'eureka' moment, when I say,

'Yes, you are right. The school thing is wrong.'

Which means one of my best friends thinks that the story of the children is false. Though it is incredibly reassuring that he has come on what he obviously thinks is a wild goose chase to keep me company but in my heart I measure up the size of the loss if my story of the march back is untrue.

We head to the last pit of the day North Gawber, over the colliery now stands a Co-op superstore. We drive along the High Street and suddenly see the North Gawber Colliery Sports and Social Club, and on the wall is a Perspex sign with exactly the same design as my badge. North Gawber NUM, except it now says 'Sports and Social Club'.

'Pull over, pull over,' I say.

We pull over and park and as I get out the club's steward emerges, a woman with short hair, short leather jacket and a stare that has stopped a thousand drunks.

'You can't park here if you're shopping.'

'I'm not shopping, I'm doing a project on the miners' strike and there was a lad at this pit who gave me a badge ...'

'Come in love, come in.'

We go into the club and she says,

'What's it about?'

'At the end of the strike I was given a badge ...'

Peter jumps in,

'My badge, my badge were given to a Tory, can you believe that a member of the NUM gave my badge to a Tory ...'

I say,

'Sorry, this has gone on for thirty-two years ...'

'Rightly so. An injury is an injury to all ...'

She says,

'If it's about a badge I'll give you one.'

She goes behind the bar, produces a metal tin and brings out an enamel badge. It has 'Sports and Social Club' under it instead of 'Strike 84–85' but she pins it on his lapel and he stands there like he is receiving the Legion d'Honour.

'Is there anything else you're after?'

I explain about the school and she says,

'There was a school opposite the pit, it's been knocked down now, old Victorian looking one. It's now Roy's Autos but you can see what it used to look like because the caretaker's house is still on at the end of the street and that used to be connected to the school.'

So we stand opposite Roy's Autos as cars and lorries flash past, trying to imagine the end house extending into a school through the gaps left by freight and white vans.

## GOES TO ONE SIDE WITH THE CHAIRS AND ADDRESSES AUDIENCE VOLUNTEERS:*

Now you will have heard of a play within a play, this is where a playwright puts a play in a play to examine themes, ideas and characters that they were too lazy to include in the body of the text. Shakespeare, lazy bastard. *Hamlet, Midsummer Night's Dream* ... This is not a play within a play, this is an audience within an audience. I am going to talk to you and you alone and ignore the rest of the audience. What this does, this creates an impression of intimacy and sincerity. I have two schools on my list of possibilities. North Gawber and Goldthrope. But in my heart of hearts I know neither is the one. I have to have them on the list because I need a method, a process.

And it occurs to me that I might have oversold the story, I might have misremembered, the school might not be there anymore, it might not exist. It also occurs to me that I have booked a tour for the show, I have had posters printed, hired venues and technicians and have had constructed what can only be described as, 'a fucking great set of doors'.

And I wonder, I wonder ... would it be acceptable to lie?

In a story about the importance of truth in stories, is it acceptable to lie to make the story better and therefore more 'truthful-ish'?

---

* The lights would go down on the stage with the exception of one set of table and chairs, picking us out. I would always lean in and talk to the volunteers directly, deliberately avoiding eye contact with anyone in the audience.

So, I am going to get your opinion. I don't want you to say anything. I want you to put your hands at your sides. Now, if you think it is acceptable for me to lie and make the story better, on the count of three put your hands on your knees. If you think I should be noble and tell the truth, on the count of three put an arm in the air ... pro tip don't use the right arm, don't put it up straight, it looks shit.

OK. One, two, three.

*VOLUNTEERS VOTE*

We need a second referendum. It's only advisory.

# PART 3

It is a big night at the Red Shed. The first speaker of the programme is tonight and it's the *Guardian* columnist, Owen Jones. The Shed is packed. Sandra is doing the door, Peter is in his best shirt and tie, George is behind the bar, Richard sorting subs. Owen Jones, the diminutive and cherubic columnist sits almost unnoticed in the corner. Someone approaches,

'Are you Owen Jones?'

'I am. I know I look like a twelve-year-old but I am.'

'Can I get you a pint?'

'Please, I don't think they'll serve me at the bar.'

Pints are purchased, seats crammed together and some of the local campaigns are here to speak before Owen. Refugees Welcome collect clothes and money. They use a squash court in a local leisure centre as a sorting centre of the donated clothes. I know some people will say, 'What about caring for British people, aye?' They have occupied a squash court, which is essentially a container for over competitive middle management to have cardiac arrests, this works for everyone. They are saving lives.

Gareth from the Bakers' Union is barnstorming the story of how,

'Wetherspoons in Scarborough unionised and two weeks later went to management and said, 'You've got the English Defence League coming and meeting here, well that's not on, you endanger our safety and it is racist, you either cancel or we go on strike. Management cancelled EDL and then they went round all the other pubs organising the workers and every pub kicked the EDL out except for one skanky craphole which we don't care if they drink in.'

Owen is introduced and starts with,

'This movement is built on the shoulders of giants ...'

He does fifty minutes without notes, which some people find impressive.

## MT LOOKS AT WATCH JUST TO CHECK

The night ends as it begins with arguments, beer and Peter selling tickets for panto.

Peter still runs an amateur theatre group in the Shed. A socialist panto, in his own words, 'Wakefield's Premier Marxist Leninist Pantomime Troupe.' And as a socialist panto there are rules, no heroine ever marries and anyone with a title has an unhappy ending.

This year the show is Corbyn Hood,* da da da da daa da da da daaah!

---

* A pre-Brexit production. I was given a walk on appearance. They wouldn't give me my lines – they were stapled inside a copy of *The Socialist* paper, which I had to read from when I went on stage.

In which Corbyn has to have an archery competition with George Osborne who misses all his targets.

The audience are friends and comrades and if we don't know them they know the ethos of the place, so it is intimate and rumbustious.

Ken plays Corbyn Hood, he is an ex-miner with a long beard and a thin frame. His wife Olivia – a local councillor – sits in the middle of the club. In one scene Ken has to go into a clinch with an actress and discuss Blairism, Ken grabs the actress and from the middle of the club you suddenly hear,

'Hey he's bloody married!'

Ken stands the actress upright comes to the front of the stage and says,

'Sorry love I thought it were an open marriage.'

'It's bloody not and you can tell her that!'

She heckles so much that Peter has to come on, 'It was as if Olivia the councillor wanted to be in the panto but couldn't be fucked to come to rehearsal.'

And each performance finishes with the Red Shed anthem, where every one stands and lifts their glasses and fists into the air to sing the song.

It is to the tune of the Red Flag, would you all stand please. I know it's a theatre but I think we all need a stretch.

*DIRECTS AUDIENCE VOLUNTEERS WHO PICK UP AND HOLD RED SHED LYRICS BANNER AT THE FRONT OF THE STAGE*

On three, one two ...

*SINGS*

*Our Labour club is our Red Shed*
*It keeps the rain from off our head.*
*So stuff your brick built Tory club*
*We'd rather pay our Labour subs.*

*So raise your glasses to the sky*
*We'll drink a drop until they're dry.*
*Though Tories Scoff and Liberals Sneer*
*We'll keep the Red Shed standing here.*

Thank you.

*AUDIENCE VOLUNTEERS PUT BANNER DOWN*
*AND SIT DOWN*

I am called to a committee meeting and it seems like a summons. Coming out of the station I cut past the town hall and head down Westmorland Street – lined with pubs and middle aged men with short trousers and shorter hair smoking, not vaping smoking.

My closest allies Peter and Sandra are not here. So I am on my own with George, David and Richard.

*ADDRESSES AUDIENCE VOLUNTEERS WHO ARE*
*PLAYING GEORGE AND DAVID:* Masks.

George begins.

'Right best of order, minutes of last meeting approved. Item anniversary celebrations. Thanks due for the previous events. Owen Jones, excellent. Josie Long well done. Now Robert Llewllyn was going to give a talk about the electric car, cancelled. No new date. Why not?'

I am sorting that.

'And the rest of the schedule we need the other speakers booked.'

'Also,' says Richard, 'I had two emails about the same Bakers' Union event and they had different times on them, we can not have confusion like this, we must have clarity in the diary or this club is finished.'

David says, 'Now, you were going to do a chapter for my book?'

Yes.

'Is it forthcoming?'

Soon.

I am left with the feeling that I have committed the worse transgression possible, I have let them down.

The next day I am 'chasing children'.

*MOVES TWO CHAIRS TO THE SIDE OF THE STAGE*

I meet Sandra.

*ADDRESSES AUDIENCE VOLUNTEERS:* Could you bring Sandra mask and sit here?

It doesn't get off to a great start as I open her car door into a wall.

*PLAYS EDIROL:*

**MARK: Oh sorry I have just bashed your door Sandra.**

**SANDRA: Bloody hell.**

**MARK: Sorry.**

She later assures me that she has nail varnish exactly the same colour as the car and it'll mend.

With us today is Ian Clayton.*

*ADDRESSES AUDIENCE MEMBER:* Could you be Ian and sit here?

Ian is a Yorkshire broadcaster and writer. He knows his local history, he knows his family history, he is one of those fantastic Yorkshiremen who can say,

'Me father were a miner, me father's father were a miner, me father's, father's, father were a miner, me Cro-Magnon ancestors were miners, the lungfish from which I am descend were miners, the big bang were nowt but a colliery expansion.'

Ian is a believer. He believes in stories. He has a list of pits to visit, a route and a story on each along the way.

When we reach Allerton Bywater Ian wants to show me the memorial built by local artist and ex-miner, Harry Malkin.

---

* Ian is a writer of some magnificent books, including *Our Billie*, which I cannot recommend highly enough. He also co-ordinated the book commemorating the Red Shed's fiftieth Anniversary, available via the Red Shed website.

It is a massive double-decker pit cage, used to hoist miners up and down, with four panels in relief showing miners at work. Ian says this about Harry,

*PLAYS EDIROL:*

IAN: He were a fitter down Fryson pit …*

They are the men who put in the props and hold up the earth.

*PLAYS EDIROL:*

IAN: … and he decided to become an artist and when Harry started, I hope he wouldn't mind me telling you this on a tape, but when Harry started they didn't know where to buy art materials, when he were a young man, but his father had a massive back and he used to take his shirt off and he used to draw on his father's back.†

*ADDRESSES AUDIENCE VOLUNTEERS PLAYING SANDRA AND IAN:* Stand up please.

So Sandra, Ian and I walk around the massive monument staring at the panels of men fitting pit bolts and descending in the cage, gazing at the twisted torsos of pit workers created by an artist who started drawing on his dad's back.

---

* Shut 1985.

† The first time I went round Harry's house, he showed me a painting of a miner underground lying on his back against a pile of coal eating his lunch. Harry said, 'I supposed that's my homage to "Reclining Nude".'

*ADDRESSES AUDIENCE VOLUNTEERS:* Sit down.

We head from pit to pit from housing estates to Halfords superstores. These are the structures that inhabit the space once occupied by pit yards. We approach one of the biggest pits in the area, the Prince of Wales.* Ian mutters,

*PLAYS EDIROL:*

**IAN: They leave it stranded and abandoned for thirty years and then clear it and put bloody McDonald's there.**

The golden arches, the symbol of union busting and zero hour contracts – a victory yelp over the defeated communities. Here is your promised future.

*ADDRESSES AUDIENCE VOLUNTEERS:* Would you take your chairs back please?

We reach Frickley colliery† in the village of South Elmsall.

We walk to the housing estate, past bargain booze shops, men playing bowls and kids doing wheelies on mopeds along the length of the street. Ian stops at what was once a school, now a business centre.

'What do you think?'

'It could be ...'

'It's a business centre now ...'

'The railings are different ...'

---

* Shut 2002.
† Shut 1993.

'These are new ones, changed since that time ...'

'Well ... yeah, it could be ...'

'I had high hopes for this one.'

Opposite is a pensioner in her garden, Ian says,

'Excuse me, love, Mark's doing a project about the miners' strike and we were wondering if you were around then?'

She says, I promise, quote,

'Which one '26 or '84?'

''84,' says Ian. 'Were you around for the march back to work in '85?'

'No, we were on holiday. I'll tell you who will know about that, Clare at the community centre at the bottom of the hill.'

The community centre has an old Victorian roof and Ian says,

'This used to be a school right here—'

But before we can finish this conversation we enter the entrance hall and at the end of it stands a solitary cleaner, mop in hand like a sentinel.

'IT'S YOU! It's him. It's you. Off the telly. Ian Clayton.'

A scrum builds around Ian and I feel Sandra's arm on my back pushing me forward, saying,

'Tell 'em you were on Channel 4.'

'So what is it you're after?' says Clare from the community centre who it turns out is also the Town Hall clerk.

'During the miners' strike I was on a march back to work and I think it was here.'

'I was on that.'

'The march back?'

'Yeah, it went past here up the hill.'

'Where the housing estate is?'

'Yeah, me dad made us take the day off school. You were on it?'

'Yeah ...'

'Amazing ... What is it you're after?'

I explain about the kids and the school.

'You need to speak to local NUM officials, local historians and local photographers.'

She writes a list and I start at the top of it.

An old NUM official first. I explain what I am doing, he says,

'I'd help but me memory has gone to shit, sorry.'

The second number can remember but if you are the holder of a story not often told, and working-class stories are often ignored, then your version of the events becomes the version of the events.

'I'm trying to find a pit with a school nearby where children sang ...'

'There's no schools on our march back, we didn't pass any.'

*ADDRESSES AUDIENCE:* I am aware I have made him sound like a pirate.

'There are schools ...'

'No there are no schools.'

'On Westfield Lane, there are two, one at the bottom and one halfway up.'

'I will grant you that. What else do you remember?'

'Clapping at the pit yard entrance as the miners went into ...'

'No one went into work that day. We had a picket line and not one man crossed!'

'But what about ...'

'Not one man crossed, not one man went to work.'

'But the picket was about redundancies, which meant men had to go into work to get their redundancy notices, come out and then picket.'

'That is true. But there were no children singing.'

'You might not have heard them ...'

'We were marching back nine deep.'

'Surely that reinforces my point that you might not have seen them.'

'Maybe. Maybe not. But it didn't happen.'

I call a local photographer,

'It's about the miners' strike.'

'Oh I took loads of photographs, at least once a week.'

'Do you have them?'

'Oh yes and the negatives.'

'To hand?'

'They are in a warehouse ...'

'A warehouse?!?!'

'There's a lot of them.'

'And you still have them all?'

'Well we had a flood ...'

'No!'

'But I managed to save all of the photos.'

'I am after the ones on the march back to work.'

'Oh that roll of film didn't come out. Sorry.'

I ask Clare for help.

'The only person who might know someone is the head of the council.'

I phone the head of the council. I say I am trying to find someone to talk to who might have seen children singing in a playground on the march back. He says,

'Speak to me, I remember it as if it were yesterday.'

The head of the council saw it, his name is Steve Tulley.

*ADDRESSES AUDIENCE VOLUNTEER ON LEFT:*
You are Steve. Could you stand up, put one hand in your pocket, feet apart and pull your shoulders back?

Steve is an ex-NUM official, after the miners had gone back to work he lead a wildcat strike, was taken to court and fined ¼ million, he is only just straight from it. He is leader of South Elmsall Council and on Wakefield District Council – he was thrown off the Labour group for opposing cuts, he is only just back on.

I ask about the children singing on the march back and he says,

*PLAYS EDIROL:*

STEVE: Oh I can remember it as clear as it were yesterday. I can remember setting off and I can show you today where we set off from and where we walked and where we went to. We passed two schools, we passed a school on the right hand side which is now our community centre ...

This is the community centre that Clare works in, that is our school.

*PLAYS EDIROL:*

STEVE: ... and Jean Elliott was the school teacher there, and she was crying on the wall is the school teacher. I can remember it as if it were yesterday.

Steve knows the school teacher who led the children into the playground and I ask if he will approach her so we might talk.

*MOVES TWO CHAIRS TO CENTRE*

*ADDRESSES AUDIENCE VOLUNTEER:* Would you be Jean please and sit here?

*MT GETS A TRAY WITH TEAPOT AND CUPS AND SAUCERS, PLACES IT IN FRONT OF CHAIRS, POURS TEA INTO CUPS AND GETS EDIROL AND HIS OWN MASK. THEN SITS NEXT TO AUDIENCE VOLUNTEER PLAYING JEAN*

Jean Elliott, two L's and two T's, lives fifteen minutes from where she was a deputy head in Westfield Lane. She is now eighty-four and has an exercise bike in her front hall. I have bought her chia seeds as she has started a new diet and cannot find them anywhere so I have brought them up from that there London. She gets best cups and saucers out, which is a gesture I always find humbling, a gesture of kindness and welcome to complete strangers. And she has some biscuits and sandwiches made too.

I ask her what she thought when Steve Tulley contacted her.

*PLAYS EDIROL:*

**JEAN: I was quite surprised when Steve rang me and he remembered it. I have always remembered it. I get very emotional when I think about it because my dad was a**

miner and he died before he was sixty. I have quite funny feelings through the strike, because in one way I was glad they were going to come to an end. 'Cos you could see with global warming it had to but it was done in such a cruel horrible way wasn't it?

MARK: Do you think the North has ever recovered?

JEAN: No I don't, no I don't.

We talk about growing up in Grimethorpe, her father, her sister and how she wishes she had done more in the strike and I say I have similar feelings, that I wish I had done more. Then I ask if she noticed any changes in the children during the strike.

*PLAYS EDIROL:*

JEAN: Some of the kids you would notice they were hungry and we always had loads of milk and extra milk, we always had a crate or two left over which you gave to them.

Then she produces a photograph, a long rectangular photograph, the type that are framed and placed in school corridors, the year photo. These are children in the playground – aged 5–7, they squat, sit and stand with combed hair and smiles. Jean turns the photo over and in hand written pen are the children's names, she reads them out, Clare, Stacy, David, Gavin, Alan.

She says, you could put an advert in the *South Elmsall Times* asking to speak to the children, though I don't know how you would word it without sounding like a paedophile.

*PLAYS EDIROL:*

**JEAN: I don't know how you would word it without sounding like a paedophile.**

She offers biscuits and I am happy to accept and so we chat, of referendums, poverty, of birthdays and schools. I say, that was quite a political decision to take the children into the playground to see the miners march back, you could have got into trouble. Why did you do it?

*PLAY EDIROL:*

**JEAN: I think I did it for me really, I knew it was for the children because I thought hopefully they will remember this moment. And I never thought about whether it would be approved or not but I did it. Don't know if anyone else did it in another village but I did it. And I never regretted it, it was a special moment and I hope that some of the children remember it.**

*ADDRESSES AUDIENCE VOLUNTEER:* Would you take the seat back please?

*MT TAKES THE TRAY TO THE SIDE OF THE STAGE*

So three of us remember.

Steve remembers Jean crying, the children in the playground and the children singing. I remember the children in the playground and the children singing. Jean remembers taking the children into the playground and crying. Jean does not remember the children singing and I fold my disappointment into the hope of the children.

Some of the children have very individual names that are easy to find on Facebook, I make contact and ask if they might help, if they know any of the other children now in their late thirties who they were at school with. And they begin to talk, finding each other, some keep in contact still, some have moved on and before our eyes on Facebook the children of the playground assemble, coalescing on screen, chatting about school and teachers and adventures. But not one of them remembers that day.

Not one.

With hindsight it is a lot to ask of a five-year-old to remember one moment on one day.

But I can not help feeling that we have allowed them to forget. That we have let their history slip through our fingers, a time when their class believed that they could change the world for the better, for everyone through unity and community.

I see Steve Tulley to take his photo on the day of the EU referendum,

'I been out early and they are queuing round the block for the polling station. And that is bad news. I'll tell you why. 1985 Labour leadership walked away from us. They left us. Labour always thought Scotland and Wales and the north were theirs, and all they had to do was sort out middle England. People round here have had their vote count for nothing for years. It has meant nothing. Well now they know their vote does matter, everyone's vote matters, for the first time their vote counts again and someone is going to get a kicking.'

I go back to the Red Shed for the last time before coming up here. I'm excited because the Bakers' Union and the Fast Food Workers campaign has had a few results. Fast Food Workers day takes place every year and is global. This year I was in Glasgow when it took place and joined a picket outside McDonald's in Glasgow. People dressed in wigs, clown face paint waving £10 an hour and a union banner! And the security at McDonald's call the police, now this irks me because McDonald's structure their tax through Luxembourg so they don't pay for the cops that they are now calling to protect them. And if anything according to the Tory economic laws of you get what you pay for, if anything taxpayers should have dibs on the cops. If anything the cops should be saying, 'Go on have the first window on us.'

Of course we don't, we sing, chant, hand out union cards, feign a protest outside another branch of McDonald's and when the police run over to protect it, we all occupy a KFC.

These events take place across the world, Tokyo, LA, New York, Paris, Glasgow and London AND the very next day McDonald's in the UK offer workers contracts taking them out of zero hour contracts.

When I arrive at the club Sandra is here and she shows me the repairs she has done to her car with the nail varnish and you cannot see a single dent.

Richard is very excited, as I have managed to get John McDonnell to come and speak at the shed, the Shadow Chancellor is going to address the Shed, though whether he will still be Shadow Chancellor when he gets here is another matter.

I arranged the booking with McDonnell's office and contacted Richard about the date and Richard said,

'We have a Derby and Joan Bingo, we can not cancel a booking it would be wrong.'

So we cancelled John McDonnell and got another date off him.

George says,

'Come here for a minute,'

and leads me to the delivery ramp out of earshot of everyone else. At least this bollocking will be discreet.

'Now you, me and Richard have had a meeting and decided to make you and Peter life members of the club. There's only three of us at the moment, you two will make five, we'll do you a nice certificate. It means you don't have to pay any subs, they're only three pound a year.'

David the ex-MP arrives, 'Get me a pint. You'll never guess who's Foreign Secretary?!'

Ian is here, Ken Corbyn Hood and Olivia, the heckling councillor.

Ken says,

'You found it, which one were it?'

Frickley.

'Frickley, eh?'

Ian says, 'I had high hopes for Frickley.'

And Harry is here. I commissioned Harry to do an artwork for the Shed, my way of saying thank you, it is a triptych and it looks like a religious icon, the Red Shed is on the front and inside three panels, the miners marching back to work, the community clapping them on and the children singing through the railings.

Peter says,

'I have to admit I did not believe you when you told me the story.'

George says,

'We'll find a good place for that, up there.'

So when you visit the Shed you will see it, next to the plates, the glass case with the badges and the brass plaque.

So the story is remembered here.

I leave the Shed, behind me the Debenhams sign. I cross the road past the two-storey, white much graffitied, still shut Tory club. And I go to leave Wakefield.

Wakefield voted 66 per cent Leave, Barnsley 68 per cent.

In Wakefield, 34 per cent of over-sixteens have no educational qualifications, 15 per cent have alcohol problems, in Barnsley 33 per cent in part-time work, 40 per cent in low pay, children in or on the edge of poverty 45 per cent.

... What am I doing? ... Let me tell you a story.

When they were planning a new shopping centre the local TV interviewed people about the proposals, they asked a pensioner,

'What do you think to the prospect of a new shopping centre?'

She replied,

'They're not going to take us pound shops, are they?'

Oh Mr Gove, the irony that in a campaign so full of lies you have accidentally told the truth,

'People in this country have had enough of experts.'

Because the experts, the millionaire politicians, the offshore CEO's, the bonused bankers, the columnists, economists and hedge fund managers have sacrificed entire communities on the alter of their ideology.

Leaving a woman so poor she is worried about a pound shop shutting.

*SINGS CHORUS FROM 'SOLIDARITY FOREVER'*

Help me out for one last time, you sing and do the soundtrack.

*LEADS AUDIENCE IN 'SOLIDARITY FOREVER'*

*ASKS EACH AUDIENCE VOLUNTEER IN TURN
TO STAND WITH THE MASKS AND TAKE A BOW
WHILE AUDIENCE SING*

# PRODUCTION DETAILS

## BRAVO FIGARO!

Written and performed by Mark Thomas

Directed by Hamish Pirie

Sound design by Helen Atkinson

Lighting by Jack Knowles

Tour Manager – Paul Delaney

Tour Tech Manager – Tine Selby

Management – Ed Smith at Phil McIntyre Entertainment Ltd.

The recordings played into the show were made in my mum and dad's home in Bournemouth and my brother Matthew's home in a small village in Essex.

*Bravo Figaro!* was originally commissioned by the Royal Opera House in 2011 where it was performed as part of the Ignite Festival. The show was developed, rewritten and finished for the 2012 Edinburgh Fringe Festival where it premiered at the Traverse Theatre. The show won a Fringe First and a *Herald* Angel.

Special thanks to Mike Figgis, the staff and techs at ROH and the Traverse Theatre and to everyone listed above.

Extra special thanks to my mum and dad.

## CUCKOOED

Written and performed by Mark Thomas

Directed by Emma Callander

Produced by Mike McCarthy

Lighting Designer – Kate Bonney

Designer – Tim McQuillen-Wright

Video Designer – Duncan McLean

Sound Design – Helen Atkinson

Sound Associate – Tim Middleton

Cameraman – Richard Davenport

Cameraman – Rikki Blue

Stage Manager – Sooz Glen

Technical / Tour Manager – Tine Selby

Tour Co-ordinator – Warren Lakin

Poster design – Greg Matthews

Poster image – Steve Ullathorpe

Assisted by NUJ, BECTU, Unison and USI

Thanks to: Geoff and Freddie Atkinson at Vera Productions, Whites Investigations, Guy Taylor, Dave Smith and the Blacklist Support Group, Helen and Police Spies Out of Our

Lives, Richard Stein and Rosa Curling at Leigh Day, Hilary and Tom.

Big thanks to the Traverse Theatre and the Tricycle Theatre. Special thanks to Ann, Nick, Gid, Emily and Laura. Salut.

# THE RED SHED

Written and performed by Mark Thomas (South London)

Directed by Joe Douglas (Mancunian)

Lighting and Set Designer – Kate Bonney (Scottish)

Sound Designer – Michael McCarthy (Irish)

Researcher – Susan McNicholas (Scottish)

Production and Tour Manager – Tine Selby (Lebanese/ German)

Producer and Agent – Mike McCarthy (Scouser)

## THANKS TO:

Gilly Roche and everyone at West Yorkshire Playhouse.

Orla and Linda and everyone at the Traverse.

Mike, Warren, Sharron, Kate and Catherine at Lakin McCarthy.

Special thanks to the Committee of the Red Shed, Wakefield.

Richard Council, George Denton, Jan Samuel, Vic Wilkins.

David Hinchcliffe, Mick Griffiths, Ken and Olivia Rowley, Andy Gough, Bob Hutchinson, Bob Mitchell, Douglas Ford, Bob Harrison, Julie Marshall, John Ledger, Jilted Joe, the Red Shed Players.

Steve Kemp, Steve Tulley, Jean Elliott, Clare Baxter, Owen Jones, Robert Llewellyn, Josie Long, Matt Wrack, Mark Serwotka, Martin Smith, Mick Duncan, Leigh Pickett, Dean at Unity Works, Gareth, Ian and Sarah at BFAWU, Sal and We Are Wakefield, Tom at Cambridge BFAWU, Lorna in Glasgow and the Tron Theatre.

Nigel Pearce, Brian Wood, Darren Vannis, Mick Appleyard, Tony Banks, Ian Oxley, Chick Picken, Vick France, John Stones, Claire Gibson and Mel Hepworth.

Katherine Mendlesohn, Tony Pletts, Matt Hoss, Michelle and Elliot Rashman, Lee Terrell.

Sandra Hutchinson. Ian Clayton.

Assisted by Bread and Roses, NUM, Unison, Bakers Food & Allied Workers Union, GMB, Orgreave Truth & Justice Campaign, Unite and the FBU.

As always a special thanks for going above and beyond the bounds of friendship Peter and Gill Hirst.

To everyone who was interviewed for the project and to those who helped along the way.

Salut!

# ABOUT THE AUTHOR

Mark Thomas is one of the UK's most effective and best-known political performers. He has won awards for his stage and human rights work, ranging from the Amnesty International Freedom of Expression Award to a Sony Award for Radio Comedy AND was one time Guinness World Record holder for the most demonstrations in one day. He has written and presented six series of the *Mark Thomas Comedy Product* for Channel 4 and five series of *The Manifesto* for Radio 4. He is the author of five books on subjects as diverse as the arms trade, Coca-Cola and the Israeli Wall in the West Bank. His work has changed the law, kiboshed politicians' careers and has been performed across the world.

www.markthomasinfo.co.uk

# 100 ACTS OF MINOR DISSENT

## Mark Thomas

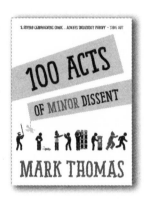

*100 Acts of Minor Dissent* is an account of an entire year spent living provocatively. From successful campaigns against Royal Parks and multinationals, to arts and crafts with porn mags, from annoying estate agents, to raising cinema workers' wages, comedian and campaigner Mark Thomas stopped at nothing.

The Acts were sometimes bold, sometimes surreal. Many brought about change and others were done for the sheer hell of it. Whether at the gates of the Saudi Arabian embassy or the checkout at Tesco – people reacted with laughter, shock, outrage and occasionally anger. Sometimes all of the above.

*100 Acts of Minor Dissent* makes for dangerously inspiring reading.